building

networks

The Academic's Support Kit

Building your Academic Career
Rebecca Boden, Debbie Epstein and Jane Kenway

Getting Started on Research
Rebecca Boden, Jane Kenway and Debbie Epstein

Writing for Publication
Debbie Epstein, Jane Kenway and Rebecca Boden

Teaching and Supervision
Debbie Epstein, Rebecca Boden and Jane Kenway

Winning and Managing Research Funding
Jane Kenway, Rebecca Boden and Debbie Epstein

Building Networks
Jane Kenway, Debbie Epstein and Rebecca Boden

building

networks

Jane **Kenway**

Debbie **Epstein**

Rebecca **Boden**

SAGE Publications
London • Thousand Oaks • New Delhi

First published 2005

SAGE Publications Ltd
1 Oliver's Yard
55 City Road
London EC1Y 1SP

SAGE Publications Inc.
2455 Teller Road
Thousand Oaks, California 91320

SAGE Publications India Pvt Ltd
B-42, Panchsheel Enclave
Post Box 4109
New Delhi 110 017

British Library Cataloguing in Publication data

A catalogue record for this book is available from the British Library

ISBN 0 7619 4232 7 (Boxed set)

Library of Congress control number available

Typeset by C&M Digitals (P) Ltd, Chennai, India
Printed in Great Britain by Cromwell Press Ltd, Trowbridge, Wiltshire

Contents

Acknowledgements

Books such as these are, inevitably, the product of the labours, wisdom and expertise of a cast of actors that would rival that of a Hollywood epic.

Our biggest thanks go to our publishers, Sage, and especially Julia Hall and Jamilah Ahmed for unswerving enthusiastic support from the very beginning and for their careful and constructive advice throughout.

We would like to thank the authors of *Publishing in Refereed Academic Journals: A Pocket Guide* and especially Miranda Hughs for her hard work and insights which led the way conceptually.

Many people reviewed the initial proposal for the *Academic's Support Kit* at Sage's request and gave it a very supportive reception. We are grateful for their early faith in us and promise to use them as referees again!

The annotated Further Reading was excellently crafted by Penny Jane Burke, Geeta Lakshmi and Simon Robb. In addition, Elizabeth Bullen gave enormous help on issues of research funding and William Spurlin helped us unravel the complexities of US universities. All are valued friends and colleagues and we appreciate their efforts.

Much of the material in the *Kit* was 'road-tested' in sessions for our postgraduate students, colleagues and others. Many other people kindly gave their time to read and comment on drafts. We are very grateful to these human guinea pigs for their hard work and can assure our readers that, as far as we are aware, none of them was harmed in the experiment.

Chris Staff of the University of Malta devised the title the *Academic's Support Kit*, and he and Brenda Murphy provided glorious Mediterranean conditions in which to write. Malmesbury, Morwell and Gozo were splendid writing localities, although Dox 'added value' at Malmesbury with his soothing yet sonorous snoring.

We are grateful to our universities – Cardiff, Monash, South Australia and the West of England – for the material support and encouragement they gave the project.

Many people in many different universities around the world inspired the books and unwittingly provided the material for our vignettes. They are too many to mention by name and besides we have had to tell their stories under other names. We are deeply indebted to our colleagues, ex-colleagues, friends, enemies, students and past students, old lovers, past and present combatants and allies and all the managers that we have ever worked with for being such a rich source of illustration and inspiration!

We particularly thank that small and select band of people who have acted as a constant source of succour and support, wise guidance and true friendship at various crucial stages of our careers: Michael Apple, Richard Johnson, Diana Leonard, Alison Mackinnon, Fazal Rizvi, Gaby Weiner, Roger Williams and Sue Willis.

Finally, as ever, our greatest thanks go to our nearest and dearest, without whose tolerance, love and hard work these books would not be in your hands today.

J.K.
D.E.
R.B.

Introducing the *Academic's Support Kit*

Before you really get into this book, you might like to know a bit more about the authors.

Rebecca Boden, from England, is professor of accounting at the University of the West of England. She did her PhD in politics immediately after graduating from her first degree (which was in history and politics). She worked as a contract researcher in a university before the shortage of academic jobs in 1980s Britain forced her into the civil service as a tax inspector. She subsequently launched herself on to the unsuspecting world of business schools as an accounting academic.

Debbie Epstein, a South African, is a professor in the School of Social Sciences at Cardiff University. She did her first degree in history and then worked briefly as a research assistant on the philosopher Jeremy Bentham's papers. Unable to read his handwriting, she went on to teach children in a variety of schools for seventeen years. She returned to university to start her PhD in her forties and has been an academic ever since.

Jane Kenway, an Australian, is professor of education at Monash University with particular responsibility for developing the field of global cultural studies in education. She was a schoolteacher and outrageous hedonist before she became an academic. But since becoming an academic she has also become a workaholic, which has done wonders for her social life, because, fortunately, all her friends are similarly inclined. Nonetheless she is interested in helping next-generation academics to be differently pleasured with regard to their work and their lives.

As you can see, we have all had chequered careers which are far from the stereotype of the lifelong academic but that are actually fairly typical. What we have all had to do is to retread ourselves, acquire new skills and learn to cope in very different environments. In our current jobs we all spend a lot of time helping and supporting people who are learning to be or developing themselves as academics. Being an accountant, Rebecca felt that there had to be a much more efficient way of helping people to get the support they need than one-to-one conversations. This book and the other five in the *Academic's Support Kit* are for all these people, and for their mentors and advisers.

We have tried to write in an accessible and friendly style. The books contain the kind of advice that we have frequently proffered our research students and colleagues, often over a cup of coffee or a meal. We suggest that you consume their contents in a similar ambience: read the whole thing through in a relaxed way first and then dip into it where and when you feel the need.

Throughout the *ASK* books we tell the stories of anonymised individuals drawn from real life to illustrate how the particular points we are making might be experienced. While you may not see a precise picture of yourself, we hope that you will be able to identify things that you have in common with one or more of our characters to help you see how you might use the book.

Pragmatic principles/principled pragmatism

In writing these books, as in all our other work, we share a number of common perceptions and beliefs.

1. Globally, universities are reliant on public funding. Downward pressure on public expenditure means that universities' financial resources are tightly squeezed. Consequently mantras such as 'budgeting', 'cost cutting', 'accountability' and 'performance indicators' have become ubiquitous, powerful drivers of institutional behaviour and academic work.
2. As a result, universities are run as corporate enterprises selling education and research knowledge. They need 'management', which is essential to running a complex organisation such as a university, as distinct from 'managerialism' – the attempted application of 'scientific management techniques' borrowed from, though often discarded by, industry and commerce. What marks managerialism out from good management is the belief that there is a one-size-fits-all suite of management solutions that can be applied to any organisation. This can lead to a situation in which research and teaching, the *raison d'etre* of universities, take second place to managerialist fads, initiatives, strategic plans, performance

indicators and so on. Thus the management tail may wag the university dog, with the imperatives of managerialism conflicting with those of academics, who usually just want to research and teach well.

3. Increasingly, universities are divided into two cultures with conflicting sets of values. On the one hand there are managerialist doctrines; on the other are more traditional notions of education, scholarship and research. But these two cultures do not map neatly on to the two job groups of 'managers' and 'academics'. Many managers in universities hold educational and scholarly values dear and fight for them in and beyond their institutions. By the same token, some academics are thoroughly and unreservedly managerialist in their approach.

4. A bit like McDonald's, higher education is a global business. Like McDonald's branches, individual universities seem independent, but are surprisingly uniform in their structures, employment practices and management strategies. Academics are part of a globalised labour force and may move from country to (better paying) country.

5. Academics' intellectual recognition comes from their academic peers rather than their employing institutions. They are part of wider national and international peer networks distinct from their employing institutions and may have academic colleagues across continents as well as nearer home. The combination of the homogeneity of higher education and academics' own networks make it possible for them to develop local identities and survival strategies based on global alliances. The very fact of this globalisation makes it possible for us to write a *Kit* that is relevant to being an academic in many different countries, despite important local variations.

6. In order to thrive in a tough environment academics need a range of skills. Very often acquiring them is left to chance, made deliberately difficult or the subject of managerialist ideology. In this *Kit* our aim is to talk straight. We want to speak clearly about what some people just 'know', but others struggle to find out. Academia is a game with unwritten and written rules. We aim to write down the unwritten rules in order to help level an uneven playing field. The slope of the playing field favours 'developed' countries and, within these, more experienced academics in more prestigious institutions. Unsurprisingly, women and some ethnic groups often suffer marginalisation.

7. Most of the skills that academics need are common across social sciences and humanities. This reflects the standardisation of working practices that has accompanied the increasing managerialisation of universities, but also the growing (and welcome) tendency to work across old disciplinary divides. The *Academic's Support Kit* is meant for social scientists, those in the humanities and those in more applied or vocational fields such as education, health sciences, accounting, business and management.

8. We are all too aware that most academics have a constant feeling of either drowning in work or running ahead of a fire or both. Indeed, we often share these feelings. Nevertheless, we think that there *are* ways of being an academic that are potentially less stressful and more personally rewarding. Academics need to find ways of playing the game in ethical and professional ways and winning. We do not advise you to accept unreasonable demands supinely. Instead, we are looking for strategies that help people retain their integrity, the ability to produce knowledge and teach well.

9. University management teams are often concerned to avoid risk. This may lead to them taking over the whole notion of 'ethical behaviour' in teaching and research and subjecting it to their own rules, which are more to do with their worries than good professional academic practice. In writing these books, we have tried to emphasise that there are richer ethical and professional ways of being in the academic world: ways of being a public intellectual, accepting your responsibilities and applying those with colleagues, students and the wider community.

And finally ...

We like the way that Colin Bundy, Principal of the School of Oriental and African Studies in London and previously Vice-Chancellor of the University of the Witwatersrand in Johannesburg, so pithily describes the differences and similarities between universities in such very different parts of the world. Interviewed for the *Times Higher Education Supplement* (27 January 2004) by John Crace, he explains:

> The difference is one of nuance. In South Africa, universities had become too much of an ivory tower and needed a reintroduction to the pressures

of the real world. In the UK, we have perhaps gone too far down the line of seeing universities as pit-stops for national economies. It's partly a response to thirty years of underfunding: universities have had to adopt the neo-utilitarian line of asserting their usefulness to justify more money. But we run the risk of losing sight of some of our other important functions. We should not just be a mirror to society, but a critical lens: we have a far more important role to play in democracy and the body politic than merely turning out graduates for the job market.

Our hope is that the *Academic's Support Kit* will help its readers develop the kind of approach exemplified by Bundy – playing in the real world but always in a principled manner.

Books in the *Academic's Support Kit*

The *Kit* comprises six books. There is no strict order in which they should be read, but this one is probably as good as any – except that you might read *Building your Academic Career* both first and last.

Building your Academic Career encourages you to take a proactive approach to getting what you want out of academic work whilst being a good colleague. We discuss the advantages and disadvantages of such a career, the routes in and the various elements that shape current academic working lives. In the second half of the book we deal in considerable detail with how to write a really good CV (résumé) and how best to approach securing an academic job or promotion.

Getting Started on Research is for people in the earlier stages of development as a researcher. In contrast to the many books available on techniques of data collection and analysis, this volume deals with the many other practical considerations around actually doing research – such as good ways to frame research questions, how to plan research projects effectively and how to undertake the various necessary tasks.

Writing for Publication deals with a number of generic issues around academic writing (including intellectual property rights) and then considers writing refereed journal articles, books and book chapters in detail as well as other, less common, forms of publication for academics. The aim is to demystify the process and to help you to become a confident, competent, successful and published writer.

Teaching and Supervision looks at issues you may face both in teaching undergraduates and in the supervision of graduate research students. This book is not a pedagogical instruction manual – there are plenty of those around, good and bad. Rather, the focus is on presenting explanations and possible strategies designed to make your teaching and supervision work less burdensome, more rewarding (for you and your students) and manageable.

Winning and Managing Research Funding explains how generic university research funding mechanisms work so that you will be better equipped to navigate your way through the financial maze associated with various funding sources. The pressure to win funding to do research is felt by nearly all academics worldwide. This book details strategies that you might adopt to get your research projects funded. It also explains how to manage your research projects once they are funded.

Building Networks addresses perhaps the most slippery of topics, but also one of the most fundamental. Despite the frequent isolation of academic work, it is done in the context of complex, multi-layered global, national, regional and local teaching or research networks. Having good networks is key to achieving what you want in academia. This book describes the kinds of networks that you might build across a range of settings, talks about the pros and cons and gives practical guidance on networking activities.

1 Who Should Use this Book and How?

The purpose of this book is to help you establish and develop the sorts of connections and links that are essential for you to flourish as a researcher and teacher in higher education. If this is the first book in the *Academic's Support Kit* that you are reading, then you might find it useful to read 'Introducing the *Academic's Support Kit*'.

What do we mean, 'networks'?

Whilst much academic work is a solitary endeavour, it can't be done in isolation from others. Research work necessitates access to a whole range of people-related resources – a critical and generative wider academic community, funding, research sites and other data, training and other assistance. You will know by now that you can't do such work on your own and are utterly dependent on others to make it all happen. Similarly, teaching can occur only when properly facilitated by institutional structures and arrangements.

By the same token, neither teaching nor research is worth doing unless it contributes in some way to socio-economic well-being or generally makes society a more knowledgeable and civilised place. Generating these effects also requires us to work with others. Students have to attend our classes and we have to find effective ways of disseminating our research findings.

The sorts of contacts we need in order to do our research and teaching and those we need to disseminate the fruits of such work are what we mean by 'networks'. Building and maintaining such networks, along with using them effectively, is self-evidently a fundamental part of academic life.

If you've read our pragmatic principles in 'Introducing the *Academic's Support Kit*', you'll have an appreciation of some of the contextual and ethical issues that, we would argue, frame all our work. Because working with and through networks, by its very nature, requires engagement with the wider context in which the university is situated, it can present particularly acute ethical problems. We try in this book to encourage you to think carefully about the ethics of how you develop and engage with networks.

What are we aiming at?

We aim to help you to acquire the skills that will enable you to develop:

- Worldwide academic networks.
- The ability to work in partnership with a wide range of non-academic organisations and individuals.
- Links with the media.

Mapping on to this, we talk about three different sorts of interrelated networks:

- *Academic networks.* Examples of these include: the people within your discipline, sub-discipline or interdisciplinary field of study; networks of like-minded scholars at university, national or international level, discipline-based academic associations (both national and international); groups or more formal organisations that focus on a particular topic or field of enquiry; colleagues at your own institution and elsewhere with whom you may work, are friendly with or simply hang out with at conferences and keep in touch with.
- *Stakeholder networks.* Examples here include: non-university partners such as government, supranational organisations, business and industry, non-governmental organisations, the voluntary sector, campaign groups – indeed, all the organisations and individuals who might contribute to, make use of and benefit from your research and teaching efforts. Such organisations and individuals are collectively known as 'stakeholders'.
- *Networks for dissemination.* Examples here include conference and workshop circuits, editors of academic journals, email discussion groups, academic message boards, electronic conferencing, the popular media, professional bodies and associations. Many stakeholders can also constitute important networks for dissemination.

Networks can exist at local, national and international levels, often simultaneously. What's more, there is usually a high degree of overlap between networks at all levels. This geographical and social complexity can be enriching and dynamic if you use it the right way.

Why might you find this book useful?

This book will be especially useful for you if you are:

- *A research student of some sort.* You may be at the beginning of your research career and will need to connect with fellow research students and academics at your own and other universities who are in the same or similar intellectual 'spaces'. This will enable you to get to know their work and them to get to know yours. Such networks help you to feel a sense of belonging in your particular academic 'corner' and give you a sense of place there. These networks can be quite affirming – giving you reassurance that you are 'on the right track'. Finally, networks are important in giving you access to additional resources, such as support and advice that you might not have available locally.
- *Someone in their first academic job.* This may be your first 'proper' job or you may have made a recent career change. Either way you may well need to build the sort of networks and relationships that are necessary for your new career.
- *Someone who is a casual (sessionally or hourly paid) teacher in a university* who would like to develop an academic career in the full sense. In your particular case, networks will be essential to getting a foothold on the academic career ladder.
- *Someone who has been in post for a long time* but whose networks are more local than national or global and who needs to make the next career step. It may be that your teaching load or family responsibilities have previously impeded you from doing this.
- *Someone who lacks self-confidence, assertiveness or an outward-going disposition.* This book will give you basic information and strategies that will help you to overcome these real hurdles.
- *A more experienced academic* who is mentoring someone in one or more of these categories.

You may want to:

- Develop your research reputation by achieving a wider audience for your work.
- Get to know better the 'users' of your research and teaching work in order to give it a better 'resonance' outside academic circles.
- Understand better the intellectual communities that you want to belong to and the place of your research and teaching within them.
- Connect with organisations that might help you with access or funding for your research and which you might want to help with their work.
- Develop your teaching by gaining a better understanding of what other teachers are doing or what is happening in the wider world.
- Utilise the media to disseminate and promote your research.
- Get yourself better known and widen your circle of contacts in order to enhance your job prospects.

Whatever your motives in reading this book, you've almost certainly already got some of the skills necessary to do that kind of work.

First of all, we want to introduce you to some types of people who might find this book useful.

Bongani is a professionally trained fifty-three-year-old who has just come to university for the first time as a research student. He understands how the business world works, but universities are a mystery to him. Consequently he is extremely anxious about being in such an alien environment. He appreciates that, in order to build a successful career as an academic in the short time available to him, he must build a whole new set of relationships within and beyond his institution and understand how his new 'eco-system' works.

Carmen is a senior academic who has published widely and whose work is well known and respected internationally. She has good networks in Canada, where she lives and works. However, her domestic responsibilities have prevented her from putting herself out and about internationally. Consequently, whilst people know her published work, they do not know her personally. This causes her problems when she needs to name referees for her job, promotion and research funding applications.

Ewan has been an academic for many years and has recently started a PhD in order to develop himself as a researcher. In terms of his PhD he is doing everything right and has started to publish from his research at a very early stage. He has one major problem: he is apprehensive about travel and leaving home. This is preventing him from going to important conferences and presenting his very good work at them.

Nancy has been working at a university as a casual hourly paid lecturer for five years. She is a graduate of the same institution. She is now taking a research degree that she hopes will lead to a permanent post. The only university world she knows is the one she was taught at and now teaches in. She has great social skills and confidence and needs to use them to help her to widen her professional world and enhance her job prospects.

2   Networking Basics

In this chapter we deal in some detail with what networks are, and with their importance, and offer basic advice on some key do's and don'ts. Additionally, we deal with the ethics of networks and alert you to a number of intellectual property rights issues.

Networking in context

Contrary to the myth of the ivory tower, universities have always been part of the wider community and society. At the same time, academic freedom has always been essential to independent critical enquiry, and this has meant that universities as institutions have had to maintain a certain distance from that which they study. Robert Merton, a scientist writing in the 1940s, emphasised the need for academic science to be done in what he called 'the independent republic of science'. We think that this principle should be extended to all fields of academic enquiry. In such contexts, the relationship between the academy and wider society has traditionally been based on trust and has generated a sort of implicit social contract in which academics generate knowledge for the public good in return for resources and rewards such as status and prestige.

However, the increasing pressure on universities generated by cuts in public spending and the economic imperatives of the global knowledge economy to turn knowledge into a tradable asset have altered this relationship. It has been recast in commercial-contractual terms. This means that there can be considerable pressure on academics to adopt particular sorts of connections with the world beyond their own institution. The outside world is increasingly perceived as consisting of a set of potential business partners and other universities/academics/ countries as business competitors. Governments encourage universities to think in this way, sometimes quite forcefully through funding mechanisms, and increasingly universities are establishing commercial divisions and appointing people to liaise with the business world and to make money out of such links. Alongside this, universities now devote considerable resources to marketing their courses and the consulting and research capabilities of their academic staff.

Academics may be torn between the competing imperatives of the more traditional social contract and public good role and this commercialisation. There is a popular rationalising discourse promoted by people such as Michael Gibbons which asserts that universities and other knowledge-producing institutions can maintain their independence and disinterestedness whilst at the same time servicing commercial business customers. We encourage you to recognise this discourse as a snare and a delusion. It is inevitable that changing the relationships that frame knowledge production will change the nature of the knowledge produced. No disciplines are immune from these pressures. Many are thinking about how to reconfigure them as a result.

As an individual you must be able to negotiate successfully between these competing imperatives. This is far from easy; the moral agendas associated with it are highly ambiguous and you can be subject to a lot of unwelcome pressure from your employer. While on the one hand you may well do such things as take on consultancies in return for cash or access to research material, it's important to keep your integrity and sense of purpose as an academic. In other words, you should engage in the networks that contribute to your work and that you feel are worth making your own contribution to, in preference to those that are merely instrumental.

Having voiced lots of cautions, we would like to identify the various networks and explain why they are important.

Networking benefits

Academic networks

As we said in Chapter 1 these are networks that you may form with colleagues within your own institution and with colleagues from other disciplines, universities or researchers in other types of organisation. The potential benefits of these networks include the following:

- Networks within your own institution are obviously vital to your work as an academic and also to your well-being and everyday survival.

- Academic networks provide you with sources of peer esteem alternative to the (possibly managerialist) hierarchies of your own institution. One benefit here is that if you don't share the values and aspirations of those people in your own institution, such networks can give you the affirmation that you need and a sense of being valued. Further, external networks can feed back positive narratives to your institution on your performance, encouraging your institutional colleagues to reassess their view of you.
- They assist you in the dissemination of your ideas, get you connected with others with similar interests and provide timely access to new ideas. This can be very motivating and stimulating.
- Collaborative work between academics from different disciplines or institutions facilitates the pooling of resources such as research expertise, ideas, funds and research materials. This can be a productive and creative way to work
- Extensive networks provide you with a wide range of potential research collaborators. This allows you the important freedom to choose who you work with. Valuable personal friendships are built and sustained in this way. Such networks may also provide you with valuable and prestigious opportunities for international comparative work.
- The wider your networks, the more people you will have available to provide references for your applications for research grants, promotions, new positions and so on. It is therefore wise to get yourself known across the range of the academic hierarchies in your field.
- As a supervisor, your networks will be very helpful to your PhD students (see *Teaching and Supervision*), whom you should encourage to make good use of them.
- Building up a network of international contacts can lead to invitations to visit universities abroad on study leave, give keynote addresses at conferences, join editorial boards, participate in international collaborative research projects, apply for new posts and suchlike. Not only does this help your work, it also provides valuable evidence of your international standing as an academic. This kind of reputation is useful when you apply for funding, promotion, new jobs and so on.
- Making contact with researchers at other universities, especially when they are abroad, can be invaluable in widening your experience and understanding of a range of research cultures and styles.

You can feed much of this back to your own institution, thereby broadening perspectives and understandings of teaching and research. Where this cross-fertilisation doesn't occur, universities, their staff and their research work can become introspective and parochial.

- Networking with academics from other disciplines or universities can also usefully enhance your own teaching practice. If you have good contacts you can swap teaching materials, ideas for classroom practice and reading lists.

Stakeholder networks

As we said in Chapter 1, stakeholder networks include those organisations and individuals that may either help you out with your research in some way or benefit, directly or indirectly, from it. The potential benefits to be derived from such networks will vary, but in general, they include the following:

- If you are in a professionally oriented faculty, such as education, business, health sciences or law, networking with external professional groups can be essential to your credibility as a teacher and researcher as well as being necessary to keep you well informed.
- Universities are increasingly required to diversify their funding base across a range of external bodies. Therefore maintaining good working relations with such potential funders is obviously very strategically important.
- Networks with relevant stakeholders will help you to evaluate the wider social, economic or political impact of your research. The logic here, which may sometimes be flawed, is that if such groups give your work an audience then it must be good. Increasingly, funding bodies expect you to demonstrate the impact of your previous work.
- Good relations with such organisations can be useful in opening doors for your research projects if you have their endorsement and support. For instance, such bodies may be happy to provide enthusiastic letters of support to accompany your funding applications. Similarly, people from whom you are seeking research data may be more willing to participate in a study if it carries this kind of support.

- Networks with funding agencies allow you to keep abreast of current opportunities and changes in their funding strategies and orientations. This may well help you to 'keep ahead of the game' as you factor such information into your forward research planning.
- Research can make important differences to the real world. Sometimes, people undertake research as active participants in these networks in order to achieve political objectives. Alternatively, lobby groups may employ other people's research even though it was not undertaken with them directly in mind.
- Many academics understand their research as producing knowledge that will assist certain causes or peoples. For this reason, advocacy or campaigning groups sometimes fund or otherwise assist with research into issues of concern to them.
- For some individual academics, such networks and their membership of them are an important expression of their academic identity and they derive great satisfaction from the work that they do with them.

Networks for dissemination

As we said in Chapter 1, these networks are those that help you to get your stuff out and about. The benefits of establishing and maintaining such networks include the following:

- The research community functions on the basis of mutual communication between participants. If you do not participate in such communication by disseminating your work, you are not a member of the research community in the full sense.
- Dissemination is, ultimately, the way in which academics build their reputation. No-one will think you are great if they have never read/heard of your work.
- Universities have an important role as knowledge-disseminating as well as knowledge-producing institutions. There is little point in producing knowledge if you don't share it. Your work will have no impact if you don't 'get it out there'.
- Academics have an important social role as free thinking and disinterested commentators on public life. This is usually called being a 'public intellectual'. We are sure that you can think of respected academics in your own country who appear regularly in

the press or other public forums, commenting on important social issues of the day.

- By disseminating your work you alert other people to it, inform discussion and debate and consequently further develop your networks.

Networking perks and quirks

Networking sounds like, and indeed is, hard work. The compensation is that it can bring with it significant personal benefits. We like it because we make a lot of friends, meet interesting people, go to all kinds of cool places, travel abroad and wine and dine a lot.

Networking activities require the investment of significant resources. The types of 'capital' necessary to support networking are multifarious – we'll go through each of them in turn.

- *Human.* These resources include colleagues who appreciate what needs to be done and with whom you have a mutually beneficial working relationship. They can help with building your networks, and you theirs.
- *Organisation.* Networking is a complex activity and requires a lot of basic organisation skill and capacity. So you really need good support staff – the best you can muster. If you're a good networker, you keep good records, keep your promises to deliver and do things and have all necessary information at your fingertips. This can be massively facilitated by a good administrator to help you.
- *Intellectual.* To network successfully you need to be up to date and interested in current thinking in your specialist field. This means that you need to devote serious time and energy to reading, thinking and talking/debating with others.
- *Cultural and social.* You'll need a stimulating atmosphere with people who thrive on the work of knowledge production, circulation and consumption.
- *Time.* Time is probably the scarcest of scarce resources, but is absolutely vital for networking. You need the time to speak to people, maintain email contact and so on, and this needs to be factored into your planning.
- *Money.* Another scarce resource, but one that you can't manage without. You need access to funds both for going to places (like conferences) and to bring people to you.

If you need to justify this investment of resources, either to yourself or to your university, it's worth remembering that networking attracts:

- Reputational benefits for you and your university.
- Income for research, scholarships, postdoctoral fellowships, research and support staff.
- New academic staff of calibre to your department.
- Visiting scholars and speakers.
- Good students.

What does a good networker look like?

Some people have a better aptitude for networking activities than others. However, like any other skill, you can learn how to do it well and success doesn't depend entirely on innate personality traits. Some qualities that you are already likely to possess as an academic are also key to becoming an effective networker. We list some of these below.

- *Good interpersonal and communication skills.* Skilled and experienced teachers will have honed these in relation to their teaching.
- *High levels of awareness of the environments in which you are operating.* Fortunately, research is an activity that often requires this sort of sensitivity.
- *A good communicator.* People engaged in research and teaching activities are usually pretty enthusiastic communicators. Academics are keen to tell other people about their work and interests and to hear what they have to say.
- *Active listening skills.* Most academics have a keen sense of natural curiosity – this is often what attracts them to the work in the first place.

You can utilise these skills in a wide range of activities and behaviours that will help you to develop and sustain useful networks. We've listed below some of the sorts of things that really effective networkers do. Whilst the list is long, and you shouldn't think that you have to be an expert practitioner in everything, you might use this list to reflect on the sorts of activities that you may undertake. So, good networkers:

- *Put themselves out personally in order to build the links they think necessary.* This involves really making an effort – perhaps collecting people from airports or enduring boring dinners and so on. Networkers will also be good at taking the social initiative – introducing people and generally acting as the social 'oil' by smoothing the edges of conversations.
- *Take the initiative and make the most of the opportunities available to them.* This means always being alert to opportunities and building on them. For instance, you might hear that someone whom you want to meet is coming to town and contact them to arrange to meet up with them.
- *Have good presentational skills, the ability to put points across well and to make people interested in what they have to say.* Don't be too flash, but a touch of real professionalism in such matters is most likely to make people take notice of what you are trying to get across.
- *Have a genuine interest in other people and their work.* Networking is not about self-publicity or other forms of self-aggrandisement. Good networking is about genuine engagement with others, hopefully to some form of mutual benefit. Successful networkers are able to see connections between people, issues and topics that may be invisible to others.
- *Appear comfortable and competent in a wide variety of milieus.* We say 'appear' quite deliberately – everyone has their own self-doubts and moments of real lack of confidence. Good networkers don't let this show and actively work at overcoming these entirely natural inhibitions.
- *Are willing to take risks and deal with rejection.* Everyone can feel hurt if people don't have time for them, but they rise above it.
- *See networking as an important activity and build it into their everyday lives.* Networkers treat this work as habitual and it is carefully planned and executed.
- *Understand systems and organisations.* Its important to develop an almost intuitive understanding of how places work and make creative use of that knowledge. In short, good networkers know how to pull strings and get things done.
- *Keep good records of the people they meet and their contact details.* The skilled networker will have an enviable address book. They will usually have good systems for keeping information, which make it easy for them to follow people up without trawling though desk drawers full of old chocolate wrappers and dead packets of crisps for copies of people's cards.

Alison is a senior academic with extensive academic, professional and personal networks. She goes out of her way to connect with people wherever she goes and always follows up all the contacts she makes. Upon arrival in any new environment, she immediately introduces herself to a wide variety of groups, she remembers everybody's names and where they 'fit' into their organisations. She is very sociable and regularly entertains colleagues. She is an energetic correspondent and keeps in touch with people over sustained periods. This means that people regard her warmly and will often choose to include her in their work activities. People will also often agree to undertake tasks that help her in her work.

In contradistinction to the good networker, poor ones are often quite unproductive, doing all or some of the following things:

- They become networking bores, talking endlessly to everyone they can find about their own interests without listening to or thinking about the other person and their projects.
- Poor networkers forget the people they have met. No-one can remember all names and all faces, but usually people are good at one or the other. These people can do neither and also may have no social skills that enable them to deal with it in ways that don't offend. We all know the person who never remembers us and whom we have thus been introduced to several times in response to their blank stare.
- They may be obsequious around 'big names', hanging on to their every word and imposing their own company on those they regard as important. These people only network 'up'. Don't be a groupie.
- The reverse of the groupie is the person who networks only with their immediate peers. You need to network with people across the spectrum. Senior people should network with junior people and *vice versa*. Networking is imbued with power relations and good networkers are sensitive to this and can handle it successfully.
- Poor networkers may be full of good intentions, but fail to follow through because they become paralysed by anxiety and self-doubt in social situations with people they don't know. Such people either over-rely on their immediate colleagues and friends to carry them through or they move into an avoidance mode and simply stop trying.
- They may allow themselves to be put off by a single 'bad' experience of something like a conference and therefore refuse to engage in such

activities any further. Such people may need help in getting back on their networking feet – for instance, a mentor might arrange for a number of their colleagues to go to a conference with them, with a brief to make sure that they're okay.

- Their interest in other people is, or appears to be, purely instrumental and only related to their careerist ambitions. Such networking endeavours are bound to fail. For instance, there is nothing more off-putting at conferences than talking to someone who makes little eye contact because they are scanning the rest of the room for more 'important' people to talk to.

Henry Evans likes to network but does it poorly. Ruth had just arrived in her new university when she got a voicemail from an unknown secretary saying that 'Professor Evans would like to meet you at 10 a.m. on the 9th of April'. Ruth was perplexed and somewhat taken aback by this imperious invitation. She rang the secretary and first of all ascertained that Professor Evans was not a member of the senior management of the university. Having established that he was indeed her peer, she enquired of the secretary why Professor Evans had issued the 'invitation'. She was told that Professor Evans was new to the university and that he had asked his secretary to arrange meetings with all the people he wished to meet. Ruth suggested that the secretary should inform Professor Evans of her room number and phone extension and her willingness to join him for coffee at her convenience. Henry did get in touch with Ruth and even bought the coffee. Ruth found his personal style quite offensive because she did not like being summoned in that way. She was further alienated by his delegation of a personal social task to a secretary.

Of course, if you never try to network then you'll never succeed. No pain, no gain.

Handy hints for novice networkers

- Networking is time-consuming and you need to balance the benefits against your other work commitments such as teaching and research. Remember that you can't network if you have nothing to bring to the network party.

- Similarly, time spent networking can eat into your personal time for family and friends. A lot of networking happens outside normal working hours – time that your family and friends have a legitimate claim on. Furthermore, it's not good for you to work all the time. Remember, all work and no play makes Jack and Jill dull boys and girls – and probably dull networkers too.
- At times the level of effort and the types of things that you have to do when networking can be a serious drain on your energies and enthusiasms. Again, keep it in balance and remember that even boring work can sometimes have long-term pay-offs.
- When networking with stakeholders, remember that their time frames and time scales may not be congruent with your own. In practical terms, this can mean that you will have to mutually adjust and align your expectations of what can be achieved and when. For instance, you may have to explain to a stakeholder your immovable commitments, such as teaching.
- When networking with stakeholders, there is often considerable demand for you to undertake consultancy work. It's important to keep a balance between your consultancy work and your research, remembering that consultancy is not the same thing as research. Most important of all – the very best consultancy is firmly grounded in solid research.
- Networking with stakeholders can be a good way to gain access to people, institutions and materials that you may need for your research. This obligates you, formally or informally, to do bits of consultancy work or otherwise help the stakeholder out with your expertise. However, whilst reciprocity is an essential characteristic of networking, you don't necessarily have to accede to every expectation, as these may be unreasonable.

Timothy was successful in gaining a government research contract to look at the operation of trade policies. He was a good networker and, over the course of the project, he built up productive and positive relationships with the civil servants in the Trade Ministry. From time to time, they had some complex problem on which they would seek Timothy's professional opinion. Usually this took the form of chatting to him about the issue briefly over a cup of coffee or lunch when he

▶

▶ was at their offices. He was happy to oblige and this also helped to strengthen his networks. However, one day an anxious civil servant rang him at the university and explained that they had a crisis and that an urgent report had to be with the Minister by the following day. Timothy was asked if he would draft it. Timothy recognised that this was imposing on his goodwill and, furthermore, he had a heavy teaching day ahead of him. He apologised to the civil servant and explained that he was unable to do as requested because of his other commitments. He also suggested to the caller that he would be happy to talk about the possibility of a consultancy contract that would allow the Ministry to call on his services a certain number of times a year.

In conclusion, what we have done so far in this book is alert you to the different types of networks that you might participate in, identified various benefits and limitations that networks can offer. In the next chapter we deal with three substantial networking issues that you need to be alerted to: ethics; intellectual property rights; and planning for networking.

Meanwhile, we'll leave you with some golden networking rules.

- Don't just be on the take.
- Reciprocity is important. You must pay back favours.
- Generosity repays itself.

3 Thinking through Networks

In this chapter we help you think through three of the more complex issues that arise in relation to networking. You need to address working ethically, who owns the fruits of networked labour and, finally, planning your own networking. These topics are linked in the sense that if you don't pay careful attention to them, they may well come back and bite you.

Ethical networking/networking ethics

Because of the complex relationships implied, networking activities can generate a lot of ethical dilemmas and challenges for academics. Here are some examples of what we mean:

- You have agreed to meet somebody at a conference at their request. It is not a meeting you are particularly looking forward to and you're unsure what's in it for you. Subsequently you get an invitation, from someone who you really want to meet, at exactly the same time. What do you do?
- You are doing academic research that necessitates networking with people in a government department that is a major stakeholder in your work. The officials in the department offer you a significant consultancy fee (which would be yours to keep personally) if you do some work for them that will assist the government's policy objectives. The trouble is that you disagree on moral grounds with those policies. You know that the government will be trading on your research reputation in using your work. Such situations require a delicate balancing act between staying true to your own moral beliefs and ethical values, whilst at the same time not offending your stakeholders.

- You have done some research that has caught the attention of the media. A journalist wants to run a story about your work, but is quite insistent that you name the organisations that were respondents in your research. This would breach the assurances of confidentiality that you gave to the organisations. Even so, you do want the media to cover your research.

Academics are, or should be, accustomed to considering the ethical dimensions of research work. Indeed, universities often have procedures, committees or guidelines to instil, enforce or regulate ethical practice in research. Networking presents its own significant and substantial ethical issues, but these are rarely discussed and are seldom the subject of any formal procedures. The absence of informal discussion or formal governance means that it is imperative to keep your ethical antennae extended.

Much of what we mean by ethical networking is implicit in what we've already said about reciprocity. That is, you should not be purely instrumental or exploitative and must be sensitive to power relations. Faustian bargains are never a good idea, and you should not use your networks to improper personal or professional advantage.

John is a professor who does a great deal of consultancy for the New Zealand government. One of his part-time doctoral students is a senior civil servant who, on occasion, issues consultancy contracts. John accepted such a lucrative contract from this student. He presented it to his university without disclosing that the person responsible for letting the contract was, in fact, a student of the university and closely connected with him. Furthermore, he represented the work to be done as 'research'. In fact the government had placed stringent conditions in the contract, preventing the team involved from publishing the results of the work. He did not recognise that his unethical actions placed his student, his university and himself in jeopardy and had the potential to prejudice future stakeholder networker relations between his university and this government department.

Each type of network that we identified earlier – academic, stakeholder and dissemination – has a particular set of ethical issues associated with it. We will deal with each in turn.

In networking with other academics, you should try and build the following sorts of responses and behaviours into your work:

- Attribute ideas to their rightful source and don't wrongly claim them as your own.
- Ensure that you do not use your power to exclude or discriminate against people.
- Act kindly towards people and help them, especially when they are junior to you or in a vulnerable position.
- Be honest when someone who is applying for a job or a grant asks you to act as a referee. If your reference will be negative, to a greater or lesser extent, you should give the person an opportunity to find someone more positive.
- Be generous and fair in providing feedback to help people improve their work, whether as an anonymous peer reviewer or as a known colleague.
- Be careful, especially in public forums, to behave respectfully towards your colleagues, even when engaging with their work critically. In the case of inexperienced researchers, you need to be particularly sensitive as to how you couch your responses.

Miriam does a lot of refereeing for a journal that actively seeks to promote critical and well theorised research. The US editor of this journal sees one of his editorial roles as being to develop and bring on researchers in his field who are often quite isolated within their own institutions. When he receives papers, which are often clearly weak, from such isolated researchers he does not reject them out of hand as many editors would do. Instead, he sends them out to carefully selected reviewers, requesting them to give careful and detailed guidance to the author on how to make the paper publishable. Before sending her comments back, Miriam always puts her review on one side for a couple of days and then rereads it prior to despatch, asking herself the question 'How would I feel if I got these comments on one of my own papers?'

In networking with stakeholders, you need to think about a different range of considerations.

- Choose who you get into bed with, in a network sense, carefully. You will have to make individual decisions and choices about who constitutes an ethically acceptable partner for you, your colleagues and your institution.
- Do not allow your work or your reputation to be used by your stakeholder network partners in inappropriate ways.
- Be sensitive to the employment positions of people in non-academic organisations with whom you are networking. You need to understand and take account of the pressures and constraints that they operate under. This means not disclosing information given to you in confidence and not 'dropping them in it' with their colleagues or bosses.

Dissemination networks involve ethical considerations that are different again.

- You must try to ensure that media coverage of your research does not compromise any individual, group or institution. This goes beyond questions of the anonymity of individual respondents to include situations where your findings might fuel pejorative public stereotypes of certain groups of people.
- Although most media people are highly professional with good ethical practices of their own, some may attempt to distort or be highly selective with your research findings.
- Do unto others as you would be done by. Exercise sound academic judgement and be fair when you are asked to review books or papers for publication. That is, do not use your power, position or voice unfairly. It is inappropriate to use such opportunities to make personal attacks on individuals. Negative reviews, even more than positive ones, must be very carefully framed and evidenced.
- Ensure that, when you author government or other 'official' reports, you do not give in to any pressure to distort what you say or the recommendations that you make. This can be tough and may require sustained negotiation and possibly even institutional support.
- Give credit where credit is due in the authorship of any reports or other dissemination. Named authors could well include people in stakeholder organisations who have helped substantially in the

research process. However, you should resist including the names of people who have made no real contribution to the work (or the stakeholders who simply 'managed' the work) in the list of authors.

Later in this book we identify some specific strategies to address these issues.

> Laura was part of a team researching the control of drug use by students in schools. Schools were understandably nervous about giving access for such research, as they did not want any dirty linen washed in public. The team negotiated a good confidentiality policy with the participating schools, which were part of the stakeholder network. Subsequently, a TV company approached the researchers and said that they wanted to make a serious documentary and requested the team to negotiate access to the schools for them. This had the potential to be a good dissemination opportunity for the researchers. However, they turned it down because they were aware that the media exposure could have had very negative consequences for the schools involved.

Intellectual property rights

In knowledge economies, knowledge is a tradable commodity. This means that participants in such an economy need to pay attention to who owns and controls the knowledge that is traded. As knowledge economies have grown, people have increasingly sought to assert their legal rights over knowledge. Such 'knowledge' is usually called 'intellectual property' (IP) and is subject to three main property rights: patents (or know-how on how to do things), designs (what things could/should look like) and copyright (the use and publication of words, images, text, sounds, etc.). In the arts, social sciences and humanities the most important form of IP is copyright. You can find out more about this in *Writing for Publication*.

Because universities see themselves as major players in the knowledge economy, they are increasingly paying a lot of attention to these issues. This means that you can't avoid them either. Whether what you produce in the form of IP belongs to you or to your university will depend upon your contract of employment, and you should familiarise yourself with what that contract says. Generally, universities now claim ownership of everything you produce in the execution of your contractual duties. However, most allow you to keep the copyright in written works. This really isn't generosity; it's because academic publications usually make so little money. Remember that the law is different in each country, so as well as checking your contract, it would be useful to check what the law is in the place where you work. Here we deal with those aspects of IP that arise specifically with regard to networks and partnerships.

Any collaborative teaching or research work that involves academic or stakeholder networks may give rise to three intellectual property rights (IPR) issues: (1) *Research materials*: who owns and/or controls the materials used in or created by the research process? (2) *Publications*: who has the right to be known as the author of any material and who has the right to publish such materials or software? (3) *Teaching materials*: when you develop teaching materials, who can claim them as their IP? We will discuss each of these in turn.

Research materials

There are two sorts of material here. One is material that belongs to, or access to which is controlled by, someone other than the researcher(s). The other is material that is created by the researcher(s). If research involves the use of material where the IP belongs to someone else, you will need to be very careful to ensure that any necessary permissions are obtained for its use and for any subsequent publications. For instance, if you are a historian using someone's books and papers from a private archive, you will need to make up-front arrangements about the use of and quotations from them and make sure that you stick faithfully to them.

Second, the research process will invariably involve the creation of a whole host of intellectual products. These will include research instruments (e.g. interview schedules, questionnaires and so on), data (for example, survey results, transcripts, fieldwork notes) and all kinds of project documentation, from the proposal itself to minutes of meetings, sketches, diagrams, research notebooks and so on.

If you are working with others in an academic network, you need to make very explicit agreements about the ownership of such materials and how they may be used. However, if you simply share an idea or set of ideas with other members of the team without recording this idea anywhere, then you cannot claim economic IPR over these ideas, though you may have a moral right to attribution (see *Writing for Publication* for definitions of these terms). Ultimately, your best protection is to have good, open relations with your colleagues and to discuss these important issues with them before they become a crisis or a bone of contention.

Samantha, from the USA, was working with academics from a number of other institutions on a major research project that generated a lot of data, including interview transcripts. While the project was in process, all team members shared all the data generated. Publications arising directly from the project listed all the team members as authors. They agreed that when the project was wound up, any of them could continue to use their pooled data. They further agreed that subsequent publications would always include an acknowledgement of the source of the data and list the project team. However, authorship would be confined to those people who had actually worked on that particular publication.

Sometimes, on funded projects, the data created will remain the property of the people who gave you the money to do the research. This can be very problematic and interfere with your academic freedom. If somebody else is going to own the data that your project creates, you need to make absolutely sure that you are clear about what you are getting into and what you are letting go of, and carefully negotiate any use rights that you may want.

Publications

There are two IP aspects here, whether you are working with academic or stakeholder networks. First, who gets named as an author? Second, who has the right to control the contents of the publication and even whether it is published or not?

We deal with the question of authorship at length in *Writing for Publication*. But remember that, with few exceptions, all genuine authors of a text have a moral right of attribution – that is, they have a right to be known and recognised as author. If you are writing in the context of an academic or stakeholder network, you may come under pressure to include people as authors who did not contribute in a significant way to the publication. Such pressure may come from more senior academic colleagues, the funding organisation or people whose contribution to the project was essentially clerical – such as photocopying or fetching books from the library. Further pressure can come from people who are technically part of the team but actually don't do any work on the project and none of the writing. As Stavros's story, below, shows, occasionally people have the cheek to take over the work that you have generated.

Stavros had organised a symposium at a major international research conference. He was a doctoral student but had brought together some of the best-known researchers in his field. Furthermore, he had identified the theme, had written the proposal to be refereed and generally done all the conceptual and organisational work associated with putting it together and making it happen.

The symposium was a runaway success, generating considerable interest from audience and publishers alike. When Stavros returned to Greece, he found an email from two of the stellar symposium participants inviting him to contribute a chapter to the edited collection that they planned to publish arising from the symposium. Stavros's initial reaction was delight at being invited to contribute a chapter to a book edited by two of the superstars in his field. He excitedly contacted his supervisor to tell her about this *coup.*

Her reaction was very different. She said, 'Oh, please! The entire symposium was your idea and your work, Stavros. I suggest you write to these people pointing this out and indicate your willingness to share editorship with them.' Stavros took his supervisor's advice and together they crafted a polite but firm email pointing out that he had created the symposium and that his supervisor had suggested that he might invite them to join him in editing a book. Stavros was eventually able to negotiate that he became the first named editor of the book, recognising the benefits of editing a collection in such illustrious company. Ultimately the network was strengthened as a result of Stavros's tactful but assertive response.

If you are going to do a specific piece of work that involves funding from, or working with, stakeholder organisations, then you need to clarify the ground rules around publications from the outset. Government departments, especially where sensitive policy matters are concerned, and corporations, where there might be matters of commercial secrecy, will require sensitive but assertive handling in this regard. You have to respect any legitimate needs of these stakeholders and, conversely, they have to be encouraged to appreciate the imperatives on you both to adhere to rigorous academic standards and to publish your work. All kinds of complications can arise if you think you will be able to publish and turn out not to be, as Birgit's story shows.

Birgit and some colleagues from another university were commissioned by a government agency to undertake a major research project and to produce a report for government. Birgit and her colleagues were concerned to ensure that they were able to publish from the project in academic journals and to give papers at academic conferences. They therefore asked the university solicitors at both universities to negotiate with the agency to secure that end.

The government acceded to their request, but only on condition that no such publications were produced until six months after the publication of the official report. In the event, the government held up publication of the report for some considerable time after it had been submitted, delaying for considerably longer than might reasonably have been expected.

This left the researchers in a very difficult position. They had submitted an abstract for a conference symposium, thinking that their report would have been published at least six months before the date when they would give their paper. In fact, it was eventually published just three weeks before the conference began. Fortunately, because of their carefully built networks, they were able to negotiate the funder's permission to give the conference paper.

You may feel uncomfortable about raising such issues at the start of a project, but it is essential to do so, diplomatically but assertively. One of the ways in which such discussions and any subsequent renegotiations can be made easier is by having built good contacts and relationships with the relevant individuals in the stakeholder organisation, as Birgit's story shows.

Teaching materials

Universities now frequently seek to maximise their income stream by 'selling' courses, either by registering students or by franchising course materials. If you are producing such materials you need to know that the university may claim them as its own IP. What many universities have failed to understand is that teaching materials are often the product of a genuine academic collegial networking process. Academics frequently swap materials with promiscuous abandon and think such promiscuity is laudable for obvious reasons. It's creative, synergistic, efficient, economical of time and effort and therefore just plain good sense. So, claiming IPR in such circumstances is a highly problematic thing to do, as such claims fail to recognise the provenance of the material. They also fail to recognise the ways in which academics regularly network and the limitations of the possibility of commodifying knowledge.

Shamila and Naoko got to know each other as doctoral students and shared a common interest in postcolonial theory and its application to media studies. As doctoral students in the same university they developed a course in postcoloniality and the media, which they taught together. Since graduating and taking up employment in universities in their home countries, they have both introduced this course and continued to share by email the ways they have developed it. They share lecture notes, lesson plans, new ideas about readings and examples, reflections on how particular sessions went and so on. It is difficult to tell which person invented which bits of their courses. However, each of their universities now wishes to claim IPR in Shamila and Naoko's joint work and to franchise them. In this instance, networking about teaching has become, on the one hand, a very generative and productive process and on the other very problematic. Whose intellectual property is it?

Planning networking

It can be inferred from what we have said thus far that the smart networker sees networking as more of an extension of their personality

TABLE 1 *Planning networks.* Judy is a new lecturer in social geography. She has recently completed her PhD and is now setting about the task of building on the relatively limited, mainly academic networks built up during her time as a doctoral student. She does, however, have some innovative research in the field of the geographies of social exclusion. Here is her plan. As we have said, these three sorts of networks shade into each other, and this is evident from Judy's plan

Year	Academic networks	Stakeholder networks	Dissemination networks
1	Attend and give papers at two conferences, one in this country and one abroad, funded by the university Contact my PhD examiner (as he loved my thesis) and ask if he minds being named as a referee for my book proposal Remain on the social geography e-list and take part in discussions Talk to Robyn [PhD supervisor] about whether we could do a joint grant application towards the end of the year and building on my PhD work	Ask my PhD supervisor to introduce me to her contacts in relevant government Ministries Write a lay person's brief report on my PhD and send it to selected relevant Ministries and voluntary sector, explaining briefly what my future research plans are Contact selected stakeholders who might support my next project and talk them through it	Finish the three papers in progress drawn from my PhD and send them off – aim to do one per term this year Complete my book proposal (drafted already when preparing for the examination of my thesis) Use the lay person's brief report as the basis of a short article in a suitable practitioners' journal
2	Organise a panel at the national conference of social geographers Finalise and submit grant application together with Robyn Attend specialist conference on social exclusion being held in Durban and give paper there	Keep in touch with stakeholders in project work regarding the funding application. See if they will consider joint funding. If application is successful, will need to liaise with them pretty swiftly See if I can get someone from the Ministry to participate in my conference panel from a policy perspective	Write up and submit for publication the two papers given at conferences last year. Work on the book (hopefully with a contract)
3	Together with other members of my panel, put together a proposal for an edited collection of the papers. Decide which conferences to attend – one here and one abroad if possible. With colleagues here, offer to organise the next but one social geography conference at this university	If the project is funded, will need to draw stakeholders into the research. both as informants and a couple on the project advisory committee	Finish the book Write up and submit papers from last year's conferences

than just a serendipitous process. Whilst the right kind of personal approach is necessary, it is not sufficient to make you a successful networker. We think it is also helpful for people to include networking in their academic planning. One of the major benefits is that it will help you to ensure that your networking is integrated with your research and teaching plans, supporting them in a timely manner. The danger of not planning is that simply responding opportunistically may leave you running to catch up with events and that you may not be able to do what you would like (for example, in setting up research sites) if you haven't got the relevant networks in place in advance.

In *Winning and Managing Research Funding* we encourage you to develop a three-year plan with regard to your researcher identity. You may like to remind yourself of the template and then draw up a plan like the one in Table 1 that addresses each of the three types of network. Whilst trying to avoid the risk of being totally instrumental, address the question 'Which links in which networks will help me to achieve the outcomes I want?' It would be sensible to develop networks across the range. You might also find it handy to develop a list of first contact points. Ultimately you need to get a solid understanding of the stakeholder groups.

This chapter has alerted you to three areas that need your close attention. We'll now go on in Chapters 3, 4 and 5 respectively to look at the three main types of network that we have identified for you: academic, stakeholder and dissemination.

4 Academic Networks

In this chapter we describe the sorts of activities involved in academic networking and offer some detailed advice about how to participate in them, both at your own university and more broadly.

A global belonging

Individually and collectively, universities have long understood themselves as communities of scholars. Indeed, even the most solitary scholarly endeavours are nonetheless part of academic conversations between scholars. We call these communities 'epistemic communities' – that is, communities that have shared ways of thinking and knowing about the world. These epistemic communities are local, national and international in character. Academics now have a greater sense of being part of a truly global (as distinct from international) community because of changes in communication technologies and cheaper, faster travel. Academics are now more mobile as workers in the global academic 'market place' and have greater and more diverse interconnections than ever before.

This sense of belonging to a community is an essential part of an academic identity and is integral to the process of knowledge production. This means that it is simply not appropriate or feasible for you to isolate yourself in your office, corridor, department, faculty or indeed university.

This long-held tradition of collegiality stands in stark contrast to the contemporary paradigm of the marketised university where individuals and institutions are expected to compete with each other in a global knowledge economy. In contradistinction to the multi-layered unboundaried nature of academics' epistemic communities, universities have tended to put up defensive walls around themselves to protect their economic interests. Even the collaboration that universities (as distinct from the academics in them) promote, such as the franchising of degree programmes abroad, is done to further commercial interests.

This means that academics are pulled in a number of different directions. They are under pressure from their own universities to advance particular institutional interests (which may also benefit the individual) and they also need to be members of collegial epistemic communities if they are to do their academic work. In order to operate successfully they need to be able to understand these tensions, balance them and sometimes make hard decisions between them, as Nandha and Thandi's story below shows.

Nandha is a well established professor at a prestigious South African university. He developed an international reputation during his period of exile, when he worked in British universities. He has been approached by Thandi, a young academic who has recently gained her PhD and is in her first job at another South African university. Thandi has done a lot of work developing a research proposal in an area of common interest, and wants Nandha to join her in finalising the funding proposal and submitting it to a major US charitable foundation.

Thandi wants to work with Nandha and thinks that the application is more likely to be funded if she is joined by a more senior academic. The project is also likely to be significantly better if they work together on it. Further, Thandi's career is likely to be enhanced by working with Nandha on a successful project.

They discuss who should be the principal applicant and, consequently, whose university will be the institutional 'winner' of the project funds – something which, in itself, attracts prestige. Nandha is under constant pressure as a professor to continue to bring in significant amounts of research money. In addition, the project is more likely to be funded if he is the chief applicant. However, this would be intellectually dishonest. So Nandha insists that, whilst they will make a joint application, Thandi should be named as the principal applicant.

Nandha's university will be far from happy with his decision. However, he is satisfied that he has made an academically ethical choice and is content to live with the consequences.

Inside your own institution

Although networks *inside* your own institution are important they often slip off the agenda when people talk about academic networking. The intensification of all academic work loads has meant that many academics come to work and bust a gut doing their teaching, answering bulk emails and doing the many mind-numbing tasks associated with the hyper-accountability pressures of corporatised universities. They often eat lunch at their desk or in meetings, seldom go to the coffee room (which may have been converted to a tutorial/store/photocopy room anyway) and then go home again, having seen their students but enjoyed minimal contact with their academic colleagues. This is a sad state of affairs and if it is the way you are leading your life as an academic, stop it now. Networks at your work place are important to the quality of your working life for the following reasons:

- They are good sources of friendship and support. How happy you are in an institution will often depend on them.
- Such networks provide immediate and on-going opportunities to chat about various aspects of work. If you have good colleagues you can use each other as sounding boards and for sharing ideas and knowledge resources, new books, teaching videos and the like. Such corridor or quick coffee interactions are important to your on-going development as an academic.
- Colleagues can share insider knowledge about the ways the institution functions and how best to get things done quickly and easily. This includes the gossip about who is best to work with in various areas and who to avoid.
- People you network with in this way may well become reliable and valued teaching and/or research partners.
- Your colleagues can help you out if you need someone to stand in for you – so you long as you return the favour, of course.
- Your immediate colleagues can empathise when your institution is driving you mad. Outsiders will not engage with your frustration sessions about your own place anywhere near as enthusiastically as your own immediate colleagues. They may help to keep you reasonably sane. Beware, however, of falling into an ever downward spiral of mutually reinforced dejection and negativity.

- Your immediate academic network may act as a gateway to the networks of your colleagues, thus saving you from continually reinventing the wheel.

All that said, your own institution is the start of the networking story, not the end of it. Ask yourself, 'Am I known beyond my own university?' Some people do great research or teaching but remain unknown outside their own institution. Others may publish good papers or do a lot of virtual networking but never appear in the flesh. A profile inside your own university is not sufficient to help you properly develop your career. You should regard your internal academic networks as a launch pad for your external activities.

When Vashti took up her first academic post in political science, the faculty she joined was at its zenith. It was filled with well connected and internationally famous professors. Scholars from all over the world came to spend time in the faculty and the senior staff regularly visited their colleagues in far-flung places too. As a group, the faculty worked with cutting-edge ideas and were influential on the publishing and conference circuits. Along with the other junior academics, Vashti benefited greatly from this. They rubbed shoulders with many great names, often having the chance to discuss and debate with them over extended periods, sharing their ideas. Some even became friends. These contacts led to many subsequent opportunities to visit other universities and collaborate on conferences and other ventures. It was not a one-way street, as these senior professors found much to interest them in the research of their junior colleagues and the dynamic environment they engendered together. Overall many long-standing academic relationships were begun.

Even internal networks don't just happen. You need to be proactive and take part in constructing good relationships. Here is the sort of 'people work' you will need to do in order to establish good academic networks inside your own university.

- With colleagues, try to build a stimulating, collaborative, generative and innovative environment. Help to organise seminars, reading groups, conferences, staff development programmes and so on that attract other people to you.

- Take advantage of opportunities to meet people from outside your own department and faculty. A good way to do so is to make selective use of interesting-looking and relevant staff development activities, sit on cross-faculty committees (but only interesting ones) and join specific networking groups. If such groups don't exist, think about setting one up.
- Make and maintain contact with people in other centres, institutes and research concentrations within your university. Get along to some of their seminars, meet their visitors and offer some seminars yourself.

So what else does academic networking involve?

First, it involves reading widely and finding out which people and what ideas make up your epistemic community. In other words, you need to work out who you want to mix with, where you might belong and whose ideas you feel comfortable with and challenged by. Equally, you need to find out who is going to be interested in you and your work. You will thus be able to develop a global intellectual geography of your interests and field of study. It's particularly useful to know which institutions have a critical mass of scholars working in your areas of interest.

Second, it may seem an obvious point to make, but simply reading and mapping are not enough. You do need to get out and about, to strut your stuff, exchange ideas, get to know other researchers as individuals and let them get to know you. Remember that if you find someone else's work interesting, there's a good chance that they will find yours interesting too – although there are some exceptions to this rule. You will need to show initiative. It never hurts to have a bit of what Debbie and Rebecca call *chutzpah* or what Jane calls 'front'. This means you *must* do a number of things:

- Go to academic conferences.
- Attend workshops and seminars.

- Join email chat groups and research lists.
- Be a visiting scholar.
- Offer seminars in other universities.
- Invite visiting scholars to your own institution.
- Be willing to travel both within your own country and abroad.

If you've taken the opportunities to build up your identity as a researcher during your doctoral studies, all this will come more easily. In the first instance you must unashamedly plug into your supervisor's/ mentor's networks and not be afraid to contact your 'super-heroes'. Senior academics are often happy to spend time with new people, and the worst they can do is say they can't meet you.

We will now go through each of the imperatives we have listed, elaborating on each in turn.

Go to academic conferences

For those of you who have never been to academic conferences, it's worth pausing briefly just to give you a quick taster. Conferences are organisational headaches, so the people organising them publish timetables for the submission of papers or abstracts of papers. If these are to be peer-reviewed the deadline will be a long way ahead of the conferences. Whatever, the organisers need time to select the papers to be presented and put the conference programme together. This is a complicated job, so you can help by sticking to deadlines – it will also 'avoid disappointment'. The same applies to conference accommodation and travel: make your arrangements early to 'avoid disappointment'.

Whilst most conferences have published themes, these are usually ignored or people's papers relate only tangentially to them. That said, try to stay within the right ballpark. Conferences vary in size, but almost all the larger ones will have parallel sessions of papers on various themes, keynote speakers, plenary sessions, panel sessions or symposia, workshops, editors' presentations, special interest group meetings, annual general meetings of the associations and publishers' bookstalls and representatives.

There are a variety of formats in which you can present a paper. Inevitably, time for your paper will be constrained – sometimes to as little as ten minutes. At some conferences, discussants may have been selected who have the job of presenting *your* paper, adding a critical commentary or responding critically to your presentation.

Contrary to what you may believe or have been told, listening to other people's papers in formal sessions and delivering your own is not the only purpose of conferencing. Conferences offer invaluable networking opportunities that allow you to:

- Meet other people and get to know them.
- Have conversations and arguments with them.
- Find intellectual/research buddies.
- Get your work out into the public sphere.
- Have people engage with your ideas in a semi-formal context so that they understand where you're coming from and going to.
- Have your work subjected to critical scrutiny by your peers prior to it being submitted for publication – an extremely valuable process.
- Possibly impress someone on the lookout for people to appoint to their university.
- Give you different institutional perspectives because you hear about and learn from people at other universities.
- Get to know the working ideas of other people in your field, parti- cularly what they are thinking now rather than what was in their last published paper, which may have been written two to three years ago.
- Enjoy the buzz and excitement of discussion, new ideas and meeting people you may have admired for a long time.

Of course, conferences are not just happy, clappy events that everyone enjoys. They have a down side too and can, if they go wrong, be quite a miserable experience. You may feel vulnerable when you present your paper and may have problems coping with any critique levelled at it. You may be anxious about answering questions on your paper, perhaps because you might be unfamiliar with certain authors or ideas. You may feel intimidated by the people or the place – and people you admire for their work may be less admirable in the flesh. Coping with conferences in a language other than your own will be tiring and can be stressful. You may feel that people of a particular ethnic group, gender, sexuality, country or class that you don't share dominate the conference, causing you anxiety or feelings of being marginalised. All these feelings are entirely understandable and very common. However, conferences are an essential part of academic life and you have to learn to deal with them effectively.

Disciplinary traditions

Different disciplines or conferences have different traditions with regard to papers. Some require the full written paper to be available some weeks before the conference. The papers are usually then made avail able on the conference website in the forlorn hope that people coming to the conference will have read them in full prior to leaving home. Some people will read them on the plane, but others prefer to watch the in-flight movie (even if it is *Father of the Bride II*). Other traditions are that people simply submit an abstract of what their paper will eventually be and give only an oral presentation. They may, however, choose or be required to distribute a written version of their presentation in their session or make them available via the conference registration desk.

Whichever tradition is followed, you will need to tailor your presentation accordingly. Making a written text available (either before or at the session) lets you refer to materials in there and make comments such as 'There is a section on this in the paper if you want more detail ...' Making a written text available may also draw more senior academics' attention to your work – there is just a chance that they will pick up a copy and read it on the way home (in preference to *Father of the Bride III*).

Prepare in advance

Your presentation needs to be carefully prepared. Unfortunately, however good their work, many academics are appalling presenters. They wander shambolically through their paper or they read the entire text in a monotone, making no eye contact with the audience. Alternatively, they talk about something that bears no relation whatsoever to the paper or its abstract.

In preparing for a conference presentation write what you will actually say out in full, bearing in mind the length of time you have in which to say it. If you haven't had to provide a full text prior to the conference this will probably involve working out what you want to argue from scratch. If you have provided a full text, you will need to select the points you wish to make/emphasise. Either way, having a text makes you think carefully about what to say and also acts as a kind of script or comfort blanket that will help you through any nervousness. If you haven't had to provide a written paper before the conference, such a text can also provide the basis of a publication.

Consider the discussant/session chair

Find out what the role of any discussant or session chair is. If they have the task of responding to you then you must get the paper to them in plenty of time. If you don't, you run the risk of being the recipient of ill considered and rushed views on your precious work.

Watch the time

Keep in mind that people who overrun their time in their presentation become very unpopular, as they are stealing time from someone else, preventing the audience from asking them questions or keeping their colleagues from the bar.

Papers are performance

Some people just read their paper to the audience whole or in part. This is the dominant genre in some disciplines, and if this is the case in yours you will need to write a paper for being heard rather than read. The problem with reading aloud is that it is a difficult art and, equally, it's hard work for the audience to take in what you are saying. A presentation *from* your paper is a wholly different form of communication. It enables you to engage with the audience much more interactively, for example by making eye contact and responding to their reactions as they happen. A presentation should be a concise and coherent distillation of the principal points you wish to make. You might combine a mixture of reading and talking about your paper, which can work quite well if you are skilled at it. Your presentation *must* be coherent, logical and should engage the audience. Bear in mind that in presentations, smoke-and-mirrors devices will not disguise a paucity of ideas.

Think about translation

At international conferences your paper may be simultaneously translated into another language – although this is far from universal. It can be done in two ways. If you are fortunate, you will be asked to provide the translator with a copy in advance of your presentation so that they can familiarise themselves with the text, discuss any technical terms with you and so on. The translation may then be done simultaneously into headphones for the audience. If you are unfortunate, somebody will stand alongside you while you are presenting your paper and will translate as-you-go, requiring you to stop at regular intervals for them to deliver the translated version. In either case you need to think carefully about how best to prepare your paper. In fact, whatever the language of the conference (your own or another), always remember that the audience is likely to include people for whom your language is not their first. This means you should avoid vernacular phrases, slang and culturally specific aphorisms, and remember that humour doesn't necessarily travel well.

Polish and sparkle

When you give your paper, do bear in mind that many senior academics use conferences (especially the big ones) as a way of pre-screening potential employees. Therefore, make sure that your shoes are shined and that your paper and performance are well polished too.

Handy hints for getting to and being at conferences

Be proactive in finding conferences

Use all the sources available to locate the conferences that you want to go to. Look in newsletters, websites, advertisements in journals and ask around about what is going on. As you start to go to conferences your name and address will get pasted into all sorts of other notification lists and the whole thing will snowball. Good research directors will share all the conference alerts they receive – perhaps putting them on notice boards or circulating them electronically.

Be eclectic

You don't just have to pick conferences in your narrow field. Often the papers and other materials from previous conferences are left up on the Web. This means that you can assess what kind of conference it was and whether you want to be part of that particular epistemic community. Sadly, many of our colleagues just go to the big 'mega-conference' of their scholarly association rather than the smaller and often much better conferences that are more specialist. You can't go to them all, so be selective.

In the first instance, you need to be clear about the company you want to keep and who you want to share ideas with and learn from. Choose conferences where those people are most likely to be and where you are most likely to get access to them – much easier at small conferences than at big ones. Conferences that run in cycles or series can be quite a good idea because they allow you to feel familiar with the intellectual and social milieu. But don't get in a rut. You should also go to conferences in other disciplinary areas than your own and those that are one-off and interesting-looking.

Find out who else will be there

Check out beforehand who is going to the conference. There may be people you know or want to meet up with. Unless it's a small conference, you need to make careful arrangements – don't count on just 'bumping into' him or her. Swap hotel details and mobile phone numbers in advance.

Think about doing your own panel

One way to ensure that you meet the people who are interesting in your field is to put on a special panel or symposium. This can be quite daunting if you are at the beginning of your career and don't know a lot of people. In that case, it might be worth asking your better established supervisor, mentor or senior colleague with interests similar to your own if they will take part and/or join you as panel organiser. Even if you have to do all the leg work, having them on board will help get other interesting people to join in. You can invite people to be discussants.

Plan ahead

The meta/mega conferences with fifty parallel streams across four large hotels have a place in your conference learning curve. If you plan well they can provide excellent networking opportunities, and if you are inexperienced they can be a good place to get the overall feel of a discipline. If you are going to one of these conferences get the programme well ahead of time and *plan plan, plan!*

Travel with friends/colleagues

If you are anxious and really don't know anyone, you could arrange to go with colleagues from your university. You might travel together or stay in the same hotel. But make sure that you spread your social wings a bit and don't just hang out with people you know.

Seek financial assistance

Remember that it should be possible to get some financial assistance from your university for going to conferences. In many universities such funds are available for doctoral students as well as for staff. If they are not at your institution you might consider lobbying for policies to be brought into line with best practice globally. If you are a doctoral student, there are often also travel awards made by the organisation putting on the conference.

Book your accommodation early

Arrange your accommodation early, booking yourself into the main conference venue or in the hotels where you know a lot of other participants will be staying. It's really worth spending the extra cash this might involve if you possibly can because it will enable you to meet people in the bar, restaurant and lobby serendipitously. Remember, most people are in the same situation as you and will be quite happy to find someone to have a drink with, go out to eat with or just chat about the conference and other things. Sometimes the ubiquitous poor-quality conference rucksack or document bag can be helpful – people can identify you as a conference participant.

Don't be anonymous

Wear your name badge even if it makes you feel stupid. People may well have read your work, notice your badge and come and say hello. Most people have trouble remembering names and it is much easier if it is written down on your chest. It's important that people remember who you are – and for good reasons, rather than because you got hideously drunk and behaved badly at the conference dinner, for instance.

Dress for comfort

Some inexperienced researchers get quite anxious about what to wear at conferences. Wear what makes you feel comfortable, but do bear in mind that academic conferences do almost invariably tend to be quite informal.

> Solomon, a historian, was going to give a paper at a critical accounting conference. It was his first accounting conference and he imagined that the people at it would be much more formal than the historians he usually hung out with. Consequently, he went out and purchased a rather smart charcoal grey suit. He was very out of place among the accounting academics, who were wearing jeans and T-shirts as usual. He managed to salvage his pride by making self-deprecating remarks about his lack of dress sense at the start of his presentation.

Don't be the spectre at the feast

You shouldn't just be a silent presence at papers. Ask questions, join in the discussion and, if you are very interested in someone's work, introduce yourself at the end of their paper. At the least exchange email addresses – business cards can be useful here. You can always informally invite people you meet at conferences to visit your institution, and you will need their details (and they yours) in order to follow up later. When you collect other people's business cards at conferences, write down the details of the person on the back of them – for instance, the paper they gave or what you promised to send them. That way you won't stare at the cards in puzzlement when you get home, trying vainly to remember what you were supposed to do with them.

Speak and listen to journal editors

Many journal editors go to conferences (and indeed, many conferences are organised by the editorial boards of journals). Many conferences also have panels of editors at which they speak about the sorts of things that their journal is seeking to publish. It may be a good idea to attend these and take notes of what they say. You can also use the opportunity to introduce yourself to editors and members of editorial boards, talk to them about the sorts of papers they want and that you have to offer. That way, if and when you do send them your paper, it will ring a bell. In addition, keep in mind that journal editors often take the opportunity at conferences to identify papers that they want for their journal and to find new authors. It is not uncommon for editors to subsequently invite authors to submit their paper to the journal.

Meet the publishers

When you visit bookstands at conferences, take the opportunity to talk to the company representatives there. At most reasonably sized conferences, commissioning editors for the appropriate discipline will staff their publisher's stand. This is a great chance to get your face, name and work known to these people. You can find out what kinds of books they are seeking to commission. Further, if you have a book proposal or ideas for one, it's best to contact them in advance and make a time to meet them at the conference. Sometimes they will even buy you a drink/meal.

Engage with others

Finally, when you are at conferences and talking to the people whom you want to know and whom you want to know you, engage with their work before you tell them (preferably not at great length and in a monologue) about yours. Don't be too humble (but don't appear arrogant either). Don't appear too needy, too supplicant, too demanding of people's emotional and intellectual energy and time.

Other networking opportunities

We have spent a great deal of time on conferences and turn now to the other networking opportunities we listed above. Much of the advice – especially about preparation – that we gave about conferences also applies to these other venues and ways of meeting and getting to know other academics, so we won't repeat it here.

Attend workshops and specialist seminars

Workshops are usually quite small events in which a high level of participant attendance, commitment and engagement is required. For this reason, they tend to be for specialist groupings and are often invitation-only. They usually last for one or two days. Specialist seminars usually consist of an individual presentation, possibly with a respondent. They are likely to be much shorter events and may be more open. They may be part of a series. You should be aware, however, that there can be some slippage in usage between the two terms and sometimes 'seminars' are longer events with several papers over the course of a day.

It is important to attend such specialist meetings if you can, as they are likely to attract the leading and most exciting thinkers in your field.

The audience usually consists of people who are very engaged in a particular topic and you will hear their current views on things, the main lines of recent debate will probably emerge and you will be able to take part in these debates. If you give a paper yourself, you will receive the attention of a specialist group within your field. Sometimes papers given at these events can become chapters in edited books or journal special issues. As you can see, even though you may be really, really busy, it is always a good idea to go to such events when offered the opportunity, even if you are not giving a paper at them.

These events constitute an important part of the intellectual geography of your epistemic community and you may wish to stage such an event yourself, especially if your epistemic community is embryonic.

Roisin was in the early stages of her academic career and her research was in the area of taxation. She looked around for others with a similar interest but found little going on. In the end, she approached a professional institution and was successful in obtaining a small sum of money to allow her to put on a one-day workshop to bring together all those who might be interested in doing taxation research. She struggled to find participants, but eventually managed to get fifteen people together. The meeting was very successful and the scholars decided to meet again the following year, with another academic taking responsibility for organising the meeting. In the ten years since the inaugural meeting the event has developed into a well established research network with an annual conference, special issues of journals and an edited book.

For Roisin, being proactive in organising this first workshop led to her being well established within her particular specialist field from an early stage in her career.

Join email chat groups and research lists

We've already noted that modern communication technologies have transformed and globalised academics' epistemic communities. You need to engage with these technologies if you are to participate fully in your epistemic community. You should, therefore, familiarise yourself with the increasing range of Web-based facilities which enable academic networking and collaborations. For instance, in writing the books in the *Academic's Support Kit*, we have made extensive use of a sophisticated Web-sharing facility (the Basic Site for Cooperative Working) designed for academic collaborators. It has acted as a sort of virtual shared project filing cabinet and a shared drafting and chat facility. There are many other such sites and some university computing services are willing to help you set up your own sharing site on your university's server.

Email lists and websites now provide excellent and instant means of disseminating information on events and publications, as well as facilitating conversations. These are an essential aid to building the international networks that are now demanded by funders such as the European Union. We have listed a number of websites that you may find useful in the Further Reading list. Just beware of OUS (over-use syndrome), as these lists can become sinkholes of time and energy.

Be a visiting scholar

As with all things global, there are local differences between universities. This means that there can be significant differences in emphasis or perspective on exactly the same academic subject in different universities. Similarly approaches to teaching, curriculum content and so on will have local differences. It is, therefore, extremely important to find out how teaching and research in your area are done at a variety of different institutions. This will broaden your own horizons and help prevent parochialism. Equally, most institutions are eager to have visiting scholars because they bring with them these different perspectives. This means that there can be cross-fertilisation from which all parties gain.

How does the business of being and having visiting scholars work? Many universities provide money to assist you either to become or to host a visiting scholar. There are also fellowships available from some research funding bodies specifically intended to facilitate this kind of networking. Some people get invited, but it is fine to invite yourself. People you meet at conferences or seminars can often be helpful in facilitating an invitation. However, it's very important to find out what the institution's arrangements for visiting scholars are and to do so in advance, particularly with regard to office space, computing and other facilities and what you will be expected to offer. Most institutions expect you to offer presentations about your research. You may also be asked to do some guest lectures or classes and to make yourself available to graduate students and colleagues interested in your work. Sometimes it may be more sensible to choose a less prestigious institution which welcomes you and provides you with good facilities, good intellectual company and is appreciative of what you have to offer in preference to a place which is inundated with visitors because of its institutional status but which often regards such visitors as a burden and offers them few facilities or even none at all.

As director of a major research centre, Rohana was very conscious of the importance of treating visiting scholars well. She was particularly concerned that her centre should have a reputation for dealing with visitors well because of the difficulty of getting people to spend time at such centres in a poor country. She had heard many horror stories and knew that being a visitor can have a nightmare quality to it. Indeed, friends of hers had been to some of the top universities in the world and had been left totally to their own devices, not to mention housed in 'cupboards' and with no access to any facilities. Certainly no dinner or even coffee invitations had been forthcoming. Needless to say these friends were lonely, became dispirited and left, sometimes without people even knowing they'd been there.

Rohana was determined this would not happen in her research centre. So, well in advance of visitors' arrival dates, her very efficient administrator organised people's rooms, computers, email, library access and the like. They were also helped in finding accommodation and met at the airport on arrival where possible. Seminars and public lectures were also planned for them, as well as enough social activity to prevent them feeling lonely, but not so much as to impede their work. Graduate students were encouraged to link and lunch with them too. Any money coming to them was always ready for them before departure and in their own currency if required. Further, if they were too heavy to take with them, she posted various papers back to their home institution. Needless to say, many visitors returned many times, invited centre members to their institutions and ensured that they were treated equally well.

What do you do when you get there? What is a reasonable expectation of a visiting scholar? Your first priority will be to locate yourself both in your physical environment and with your new, albeit temporary, colleagues. It's also a good idea to set up a programme of activities early on. This should include a range of appointments with people you want to meet, events you want to attend, and presentations that you will do. One of the things you might do with your host is to plan a mini-conference, international or national seminar around your joint interests. Consider putting out an edited collection in association with this or a special issue of a journal. Do make sure that you balance your study leave pro-gramme between such activities and your own need to get on with your research.

We think it's a good idea to give your seminars early on in your visit because that alerts people to your presence and your exciting ideas, opening up many more opportunities for others to engage with you. This may well result in more invitations than you can appropriately handle and you need to be selective about what you agree to do. If you have been invited and partially or fully funded by your host institution, then you need to be sensitive to their expectations without allowing them to eat you alive. In this case, you really need to sort out ahead of time how much work you will be expected to do for them.

Although being a visiting scholar is generally related to research, it is useful to check out courses and teaching in your host institution, to maybe do the odd lecture or tutorial class, and to go home with some copies of people's unit guides, reading and resource lists. But you are not there to teach, so do not get sucked into doing too much teaching despite the 'kind' offers of your hosts. Of course some visits are for teaching exchanges. These can be particularly beneficial if you are able to try out new ideas or pedagogies or if you are in a teaching team which introduces you to new approaches to take back with you.

When James visited a university in Brazil, he became very involved with Javier's education studies course, doing a lot of teaching and running tutorials. He was particularly keen to be part of a teaching team that contextualised education within popular media culture. Javier's team was exploring the best pedagogies to do this and coming up with many highly original and successful pedagogies. James became a very active member of the team. He gave and learnt

▶ heaps. When he returned to his Californian university he arranged for Javier to visit in order to teach in a similar programme. Both James and Javier benefited greatly from teaching in different national/cultural contexts, as this also enhanced their teaching in their own cultures. And they became firm friends.

What should I do about my family? Many academics with families nonetheless visit other universities for prolonged periods and take all or some of their family with them. This takes a lot of extra planning and also means that family needs, like children's schooling, have to be addressed. None of this is easy and it can cut into your study leave time quite a lot. However, there are also many benefits to having your family with you, not the least being that you do not miss and worry about them. The other benefits are that you have their company, can enjoy local activities together and having a family may well help you to integrate more readily among the locals. They of course have the benefit of lots of new and hopefully interesting experiences and often make new friends for life.

A golden rule for all visiting scholars is, be sociable. Go to coffee, go to lunch, invite people to join you. This will make your stay more fun and will also help you make new academic allies and friends.

Offer seminars in other universities

You are likely to get invitations to visit other universities if you are getting out and about and have something interesting or useful – or hopefully both – to say when you do. Let us assume that you have lots of interesting ideas, so if the invites are not flowing it may be because you are not out and about in the right places. How do you rectify this and ensure that the invitations start flowing in?

Perhaps you could start by inviting yourself to visit another institution. This may sound extremely embarrassing, but it is actually a common practice. For instance, many people who go to conferences away from home invite themselves to nearby universities so as to make the most of the travel costs and the time away. And, of course, you may also suggest to colleagues at nearby universities that you could offer a seminar for them.

You will probably be aware of which universities you would like to visit and know of people or research groups there who are likely to be interested in your ideas. If you have never met the key people involved, you can contact them by email, indicate you would like to visit and explain what you are working on. In this first approach, it is helpful if you establish your common interests. You might do this by saying something about what you've read of theirs or that some common friend/acquaintance suggested that you make contact.

What are the likely responses to this initiative? Academics are usually happy to invite interesting people to come to their institutions but it is possible that your email will be ignored – possibly because the person you've sent it to is so overwhelmed with emails that they can't respond to everything or they may be on leave. You may be invited to visit and spend some time chatting. Such visits may lead to an invitation to do a seminar – and it's a good idea to be prepared for this to happen at short notice when big distances are involved. Or they may respond to your initial email by immediately inviting you to give a seminar.

You may already know the key people at the institutions you want to visit – they may have heard you speak at a conference and spoken to you about your paper or have marked your PhD and reacted favourably. In such cases, it is absolutely fine to email them and say that you are going to be somewhere near their institution and you would love to visit, to see them and to give a seminar for their colleagues and students.

The next step, in both instances, is to send some engaging titles, abstracts and a short CV. It may also be useful if you indicate any particular people you want to meet. Near to the date, email ahead to make sure of the arrangements. Prepare properly for any seminars/papers you are giving so that you can present yourself at your best. Don't be disappointed if you only have a few people at the seminar – they may be the very people you want to connect with.

It may not be possible for people to pay you anything, or they may be able to give you a small amount. Even if you have to pay for your own travel in full or in part, this might be quite a good investment for you. In some countries you might be able to claim part of it against tax, so you need to keep records and receipts for everything. Check this out with your accountant or tax office and devise a good system for keeping a record.

Invite visiting scholars to your own institution

Even if you do not have study leave yourself or are unable to go away because of other responsibilities, you can get some of the benefits of going elsewhere to network by inviting people to your own institution.

You will have to expend some effort to arrange visits and on looking after visitors when they are with you.

How do you fund such visits? They will inevitably cost money and you need to check out the sources of funding that are available both within and beyond your own institution. If you are chasing an international speaker, your university may be able to help you with funding directly or to get it from another source. For instance, the British Council and other funders have money for making links between universities in the UK and the Commonwealth. Also, travel scholarships to bring overseas scholars to your country may be available from major funding bodies – though you will almost certainly have to bid competitively for them. Most universities have funds to support the travel, accommodation and *per diem* costs of visiting scholars. Some require you to find matching funds from other sources or a co-host. Some also have restrictions on what they will pay for and what they expect the co-host to pay for. You can usually co-host with other universities or with industry partners or government agencies. Of course they will all expect their pound of flesh and you need to be clear to your potential visitors what is expected of them.

In organising the visit, you need to pay attention to what is best for your visitor. Visits will vary in length and intensity and your plans will vary accordingly. If your visitor is from near by and will be around only to give a seminar you do not need more than minimal planning – making sure they know how to get there, booking parking and a room for the seminar, advertising and so on. For long periods of study leave, the planning should be aimed at helping visitors settle in quickly and ensuring that they have all the appropriate facilities available.

Visits that will last a few days are probably the ones that need the most careful preparation. In this case it is really important to think carefully about and discuss with your visitor what they should do. If your visitor is someone whom everyone wants a piece of, even the shortest visit will have to be planned in such a way that they do not collapse with the strain. You do not want to kill them through overwork and you must leave space clear for them to mix informally without being exhausted. They also need time to themselves.

When someone is coming to visit your university, you should set up an itinerary for them well in advance. Do so in consultation with them rather than rushing ahead yourself without allowing them to take any of the initiative. For instance, they may have their own wishes about who they want to meet, at your university and at others. Nor should you spring any nasty surprises on them when they arrive. The itinerary should include:

- Arrival and departure dates, times and travel details. You need to be clear on these, even if your visitor is making their own travel arrangements.
- Whether you will collect them from the airport or station and, if not, whether someone else will meet them or where they can get a taxi.
- Similar information about what will happen when they are due to leave.
- How they will be ferried around when they are with you.

Your co-hosts, if any, should also be involved in the negotiations and local travel plans. These basic courtesies are very important if you are going to make the best use of your visitors. It's important that they know what to expect so that they can do their own preliminary planning. You do not want them to be unhappy when they are with you and then leave with a bad taste about you and your university in their mouth.

Don't be exclusive and greedy with your visitors. You can share them. Keep in mind that one of the reasons for them to visit is that they want to get stimulated academically by the work of you and your colleagues. They want to be part of academic conversations that move their thinking on and not to feel that they are simply putting in without getting anything back. So encourage your colleagues to be more than passive recipients of their pearls of wisdom and to engage them in discussion and debate.

Be willing to travel both within your own country and abroad

As we've indicated throughout this chapter, there are lots of opportunities for academics to travel in relation to their work and these are growing all the time. At the same time, electronic communication allows ready connections and links in virtual worlds, which can be easily translated into corporeal links though travel. Some people travel all the time for research, teaching or consultancies, such that they are hardly ever at their own institution. Others stay put. Both these extremes are problematic. Those who are never at home can't make a proper contribution to their own department and colleagues. Those who never travel often have a heads-down, highly parochial way of being in the academic world and have little sense of what is going on in other places and cultures. In these globally interconnected times academics need to have their heads up, to see what is going on beyond their own little world and to consider the implications for their teaching and research. The best way to do this is through travel (within reason) and not just virtually.

Travel can be costly, in terms of time, money and physical effort – just how costly will depend on where you are based and the transport links available to you. Sometimes others will pay for you and sometimes you have to fund yourself, claiming the money back through tax as a work-related expense if possible. Whatever, it is worth it. And while you are away, try to get to places that are dissimilar from your own and to work with people who come from various cultures. The well networked, global academic has to be cosmopolitan.

One of the main benefits of being an academic is that it provides opportunities for you to spend time with interesting people in interesting places. Moreover, your work and career can only benefit from well planned and appropriate academic networking.

5 What are Stakeholder Networks?

This chapter discusses the notion of 'stakeholder', identifies what and who they are and explores the sorts of work you can do with them.

Dominant discourses to be wary of

The lexicon of contemporary university governance contains a number of 'buzz words':

- Partnerships.
- Collaboration or links with industry.
- End users.
- Capacity building.
- Co-sponsorship, co-funding.
- Serving the professions.
- Applied knowledge.
- Commercialisation.
- Path to market.
- 'Mode 2'.
- 'Useful' knowledge.

And the list goes on. Many of these terms are related to the notion that universities have a wider 'stakeholder' community. Universities are increasingly obliged by government to demonstrate that they adequately serve these stakeholders and there are financial incentives to do so. Consequently your university may encourage you to give top priority to those perceived as stakeholders. There are two main ways in which this happens.

First, many governments argue that the best way of ensuring that universities serve their stakeholders' needs is to set up funding arrangements whereby the stakeholder is, effectively, a customer for universities' work. This is generally achieved by government simultaneously scaling down its funding for universities and implementing various policy processes to force them to seek alternative funds from stakeholders. Stakeholders, it is assumed, will act as discerning customers and will want to ensure that they get 'value for money' from universities.

To be successful in this area, university management teams have spawned further internal machinery and structures to secure business and thus additional income for the university. Most universities now have commercial arms and their job is to facilitate the winning of such funds from stakeholder/funders. You can usually recognise them by the inclusion of the terms such as 'Innovation' in their titles. We've even heard of one, tautological, 'Dean of New Initiatives'.

These management structures don't win stakeholder funds themselves. At best they facilitate the work of academics in building these networks and at worst they just plain pressurise them into it. Thus you may find yourself coming under pressure to produce the sorts of research that can be commercialised or that will at least be supported financially by industry or other sources. Equally, you may also be expected to develop teaching programmes that produce the sorts of 'oven-ready' employees that some employers want. This is commonly called the 'commodification' and 'vocationalisation' of the university.

Second, these financial incentives have been accompanied by a strong ideological campaign directed at the elevation of the status of the types of knowledge that are produced for stakeholders: the applied, the functional and that with a practical application or utility. This new ideology preaches that knowledge must have a 'use value' or an 'exchange value' and be understood in mainly technical and instrumental terms. That which cannot be understood in this way is increasingly residualised – that is, discredited and marginalised.

In consequence, knowledge can no longer be seen as a gift, free, disinterested, for its own sake or as contributing to the common weal. The knowledge that once might have justified its existence in these terms must now account for and justify itself in terms of the knowledge's commodity value. Stakeholders, it is argued, need 'evidence', not idle speculation or unpractical claptrap. Thus philosophy departments now turn their hand to business ethics and English departments work with the creative industries and so on. Of course, because under this ideology the customer is always right, a further imperative is that the knowledge that universities produce should not threaten their relationship with their stakeholders, so it must not be critical or political.

Within this ideological construction, stakeholders are understood in a very limited way. The university itself is not permitted to be a stakeholder in knowledge production and distribution, even though it clearly is. Neither can the term 'stakeholder' include the public, the ordinary citizens, the community or other such non-institutional actors who cannot either sign a contract or pay for knowledge. Stakeholders must be clearly identifiable, legal entities with resources that can be 'leveraged'.

The stakeholder rules, okay!

It is important to resist the imperatives that may well be dominant in your university to see stakeholders in this way. We think that it is important not to subscribe to the reductionist views outlined above and to have a richer and more robust view of the range of stakeholders available to you and a more dialogical view of your relationship with them. Further, if you are a reflexive academic, you will recognise that these all too dominant discourses divert and pervert the knowledge production process and indeed the very nature of the university. Clearly universities need to support themselves financially, but equally they must have an agenda that is more than that of their stakeholders so conceived.

So what is a stakeholder?

In Chapter 1 we described stakeholders as all organisations and individuals who might contribute to, make use of and benefit from your research and teaching efforts. Thus a stakeholder is anyone who, or any entity which, has some form of 'stake' in your work. They do not need to have paid you or your university for it. In contrast to the dominant discourse we described above, here are just a few examples of stakeholders more broadly defined:

- People in poverty may have a stake in the research you undertake on the causes of poverty and on the ways in which it might be alleviated. They have a stake in the sorts of explanations you offer and the suggestions you make.
- The public is a stakeholder not just because taxpayers may fund much of your salary but also because your work may be in the

general interest. For instance, the public has a general interest in protecting the environment even if sectional interests such as those associated with high-polluting industries do not. So research that is directed towards environmental protection is in response to the public as stakeholder.

- Students are in the stakeholder category too. As 'users' they are increasingly expected to pay for university knowledge and credentials. The climate in higher education combined with the state of the job market encourages students to see their university studies as an investment in their own human capital – that is, as a private benefit. Further, their choices of academic programme and their subsequent employment opportunities steer the directions of universities. Faculties with lower student demand lose 'load' and the funding that goes with it. This money then goes instead to those who get 'bums on seats'. Faculties and their courses may vary in popularity among students at any one time. At present, the major growth area is in business, management and commerce. You may care to check out the following website for a satirical view on this: http://www.cynicalbastards.com/ubs/. Yet, despite all this, and their vested interest in their university's research and teaching, students tend to be thought of as clients, not stakeholders.

So, in reality, you may have multiple stakeholders and their interests will often be somewhat diffuse and perhaps contradictory. Sectional interests may conflict with the public interest and some of those sectional interests will conflict with others. For instance, unions may have a short-term interest in keeping certain high-polluting industries going to protect the jobs of workers. But the longer-term interest of workers in general is in a clean and safe environment. Some stakeholders will want you to undertake work that is about addressing longer-term concerns and others will just want their short-term needs addressed. Further, some stakeholders will be in a position to pay you, others will not or may support you indirectly.

The challenge for you is to ensure that you have an understanding of your responsibilities towards various stakeholders. And students should be included here, as can the university system within which you work. Universities clearly have a stake in you making money to help their bottom line, but they also have a stake in the university sector being seen as a superior provider of 'knowledge services'. They cannot get this kind of reputation if their academic staff are in the pocket of particular commercial or political stakeholders and thus have no academic independence and credibility.

By now it should be clear to you that the notion of stakeholder networks is very far from unproblematic. For instance, how do you network, say, with the public or the poor or with poorer nations?

Who are the stakeholders, then?

It is time for a little specificity about who may be your stakeholders. Our list of possibilities may surprise you, for it is more inclusive than a list that might be inferred from the reductionist notion of a stakeholder implied in government discourses. We think that stakeholders can be usefully subdivided into four categories:

- Professional associations and unions.
- Non-governmental organisations (NGOs).
- Business.
- Government.

The lines of demarcation between these may not be as clear as the list implies and you do need to be alert to the border-crossing and hybrid formations that exist. Additionally, some of these stakeholders may form umbrella representative organisations and these can provide fruitful networking opportunities. For instance, particular industries may form national or international groupings with names such as the 'National Council of Clothes Drying Technology Producers'. Some of these umbrella groups cover whole sectors. For instance, in the UK there is the National Council of Voluntary Organisations, the Confederation of British Industry and the Trades Union Congress. We will now look at each of these major stakeholder categories in turn.

Professional associations and unions

Professional associations include any association formed by a body of people practising a (generally white-collar) profession. Such associations are designed to protect and further the interests of that profession. We don't intend getting into a debate about the notion of a profession, but the people who generally identify themselves as being in a profession include chartered or certified accountants, registered psychologists, literary publishers and doctors. Unions tend to be formed to protect the industrial rights of workers. While they are often formed by blue-collar workers, they are also associated with pink-collar work (that is, female-dominated work such as retail) and some professions (for instance, nursing).

You will need to identify which associations and unions are pertinent to your particular disciplinary or interdisciplinary space. You may be amazed at what you turn up once you start looking. For instance, in the field of school education you might find:

- Principals' (head teachers') associations.
- Associations related to school subject areas such as English or mathematics or knowledge orientations such as vocational education.
- Associations formed around age cohorts – for instance, the post-compulsory or pre-school years.
- Teachers' unions.

It can often be difficult to distinguish between unions and professional associations. Whilst associations may be more concerned with professional standards and knowledge and unions with the particular employment interests of their members, generally both types of group engage in both sorts of activities.

Non-governmental organisations (NGOs)

This very broad term is usually taken to include those groups that are not part of government, business or professional associations and unions. They are sometimes also referred to as the third sector or even as civil society. Sub-groups here include

- Charities.
- Lobby groups.
- Social movements.
- Clubs.

NGOs are therefore a wide-ranging and eclectic group and it may be hard to differentiate between the sub-categories above. Generally, NGOs are not-for-profit organisations, although they may try to generate operating surpluses to use in furtherance of organisational objectives. NGOs may:

- Work for particular communities and subscribe to broad public-good imperatives, such as peace, public safety or child protection.
- Be advocates on behalf of exploited or vulnerable people, such as sweatshop workers or refugees.
- Maintain important public institutions such as museums, libraries and art galleries.
- Focus on vulnerable nations, such as those that are poor or carry high debt burdens.

Both social movements and charities may engage in substantial lobbying activities. At the same time, charities are increasingly engaging in 'social entrepreneurship' as a means of garnering the money and other resources necessary to achieve their charitable objectives. In working in such ways, charities are said to be 'not-for-profit' organisations. In other words the surplus that is produced through their activities is channelled back into their activities. Lobby groups may engage extensively with activities designed to promote sectional interests, especially corporate ones.

Business

'Business' is also a surprisingly broad and eclectic term encompassing a wide range of activities and actors, from small or micro-enterprises to multinational corporations and from primary producers (who run mines and so forth) to stock markets (which sit on gold mines). However, these are all organisations that have the maximisation of profit or 'shareholder value' as their *raison d'être*.

Despite their profit motivation, businesses may establish subsidiary organisations of an ostensibly philanthropic nature to work in areas such as the arts or sport. Such subsidiary interests are part of what is often called the corporate citizenship or corporate social responsibility work of business. The work of corporations in these areas may be genuine or thinly disguised self-promotion or legitimacy claims. The work that you do for business may be in relation to its 'core business' or such philanthropic sidelines.

Government

Government exists at a number of levels: local, state, national or federal. Government organisations tend to be elected and to generate the bulk of their revenue from taxation. Governments are generally expected to be accountable to the general population. In addition, there are a number of quasi-governmental organisations that are either international (such as the United Nations) or supranational (such as the International Monetary Fund)

Things have got more complicated of late, as countries across the world, either at their own volition or at the behest of organisations such as the World Bank, have increasingly sought to apply what is often called 'new public management'. At its simplest, this means that governments have sought to become more like business in their principles and practices. For instance, the provision of education may now be called a 'business sector' or 'industry' and be subject to the same kind of accounting rules and performance indicators as businesses in the private sector.

Governments are often restructured when there is a change of political party or leadership. Indeed, such structures can change with breathtaking rapidity, and when they do, key personnel usually change too. New governments also try to distinguish themselves ideologically from the previous incumbents as a means of distancing themselves. Such distancing often involves a new linguistic repertoire and the labelling of previous repertoires as politically incorrect. This process may also involve distancing themselves from the academics who supplied services to the last government and who are known for their political alignment. Networkers need to keep up to speed with such changes and with the changes of ideology that accompany them. Such changes may require some fast footwork.

What can you do for or with stakeholders?

These various types of stakeholders may want to work with you in a number of ways. These include the following:

- Research, consultancy and evaluation projects.
- Professional development activities.
- Education and training activities.
- Participation in their governance.
- Involvement in their on-going activities.

We will now deal with each in turn.

Research, consultancy or evaluation projects

We discuss contract research, consultancy and evaluation in *Winning and Managing Research Funding*. As we say there, the distinction between these categories can be quite blurred.

The ways by which you might win such funded projects can vary. The funder might issue a general invitation to tender for the work or just invite a selected list of people and institutions to bid. If the funder knows you or your work well, you may simply be asked directly if you will undertake the work. If this happens you may be in a strong position, as the stakeholder may have few alternatives to using your services.

With contract research, consultancies and evaluations the funder may be clear about the specific amount of money available, may indicate a range within which the work will be funded, or may ask you to name your price in any tender for the work you submit.

The differences between consultancies and contract research in terms of the specification of work are not great. The contractor (the stakeholder in this instance) will set down the parameters of the work with varying degrees of specificity. The stakeholder may lay down terms of reference, with details of how the intellectual property issues will be dealt with.

In the case of consultancies you will certainly be expected to produce more than research findings. The stakeholder will want you to produce findings that allow you to formulate advice, make recommendations, propose a course of action, implement solutions and so forth. The funder may already have a rough idea of what the answers will be or what sort of solutions it wants, or it may alternatively give you a more open agenda. Make sure that these issues are clarified ahead of the work starting.

Evaluations involve an assessment of the merits or otherwise of an existing situation, programme or policy and can be either formative or summative. The methodologies of evaluations vary as widely as those of research. Such things as future funding, staffing, policy directions and so on can depend upon the outcome of an evaluation. Formative evaluations are designed to improve things along the way, whereas summative evaluations constitute a retrospective assessment of past performance. Summative evaluations can be contentious, as they involve the delivery of a judgement and can therefore 'make or break'. A summative evaluation may also be designed to improve things for future rounds of similar work by the stakeholder organisation, and the evaluator may therefore be offered successive rounds of contracts as the work progresses. Often the results of evaluations are confidential and involve little hope of you being able to claim intellectual property rights (IPR) and thus to publish.

Here are some examples of the sort of thing you might be asked to do. Consider how you would categorise each one.

Professional associations and unions

The academic unions are very bothered about the heavy work load of university staff and the effect that it may have on their health. Neither has been well documented, even though there is enough anecdotal evidence about for the unions to be worried. The unions want to undertake a campaign to push for reduced work loads. Len is an active member of one of these unions and is offered a contract to gather data about how heavy the work loads are, how such work loads are manifested and the effects on academics' health. His report is to be used to lobby employers.

NGOs

The major football association in Murray's home state is concerned about the future careers of its players once they stop playing league football. Many league players finish their football career quite young and then wonder what work to do. This life transition is sometimes accompanied by psychological distress. The football association is also concerned about how to assist those young hopefuls who missed out on the big time, but came close. The association has employed Murray, who has a well known record of research in the field of player welfare and also in education, to identify the educational pathways they might follow and to make recommendations about the best options available to these players in various parts of the education system. His brief includes negotiating with the education institutions to see what sorts of fee reduction and entry concession packages they might be prepared to offer.

Insufficient.

Business

Smithfield is an ailing locality whose economy is in recession, depleted by the privatisation and downsizing agendas associated with the government's restructuring of the power generation industry. As a consequence, many small businesses in the town have shut down. The town now has rows of empty shops and a depressed economy and population. The local business people have banded together to form a local urban regeneration committee. This committee has employed Steve, whose expertise is in the economic and social renewal of local communities. He has been asked to undertake an audit of the area's current and potential resources, to work with the committee over the next three-year period to develop future directions for business in the town and to chase new money for such opportunities.

Government

The government is concerned about children and obesity. The press has run scare stories about the number of young people who are seriously overweight, and various health and parent lobby groups have been pressing for government action. They have been asking the government to address the problem and also been scathing about the government's neglect of children. Although the government is unsure about the real extent of the problem, it has caved in to the pressure of 'public opinion' and funded the development of a three-month public awareness campaign directed at parents. This is about to go to air. However, the government agency is not sure about the extent or severity of the problem. It has advertised for a multi-disciplinary methodological team to evaluate the public awareness campaign. In addition, it would like this team to undertake a preliminary analysis of the extent of the problem and its causes as well as to recommend any necessary further action.

Professional development activities

Many stakeholder groups may seek professional development (PD) training for their managers, employees or members. They want and may need to keep up to speed on important professional matters and/or want to provoke discussion and debate among themselves. And they may want to employ relevant university 'experts' to assist them. You may be able to provide just the expertise they need. Hence they may invite you to do such things as:

- Be a speaker at a conference.
- Present a seminar,
- Conduct workshops.
- Lead discussion groups.
- Prepare discussion documents or issues papers.

Below are the sorts of things the people we know have been asked to do.

Professional associations and unions

Ilse is a health education expert on the AIDS pandemic and has been invited to South Africa to talk at a conference of school principals. The incidence of AIDS in South Africa is very high. She will give a keynote address that outlines dominant patterns and trends and alerts the principals to current research about the impact of AIDS on the lives of children and their education. She will run a series of workshops with principals, identifying the sorts of issues they commonly have to deal with and developing practical strategies for responding to them.

NGOs

Rhonda is an expert on the issue of women's budgets and has been asked by a major international NGO to write a discussion paper for senior staff who have only recently heard about women's budgets and feel the need to know more. Once it is complete she will meet them, talk them though the issues and assist them to consider what the ideas in her paper and the issues it identifies mean for their next round of policy development.

Business

A major food company is concerned about the many recent examples of contaminated food products. It has in place a set of risk management practices, but worries they may not be adequate and that many staff do not take them sufficiently seriously. Robert has a lot of experience of helping companies develop their risk management practices. He is also up to date with the latest developments in the field. He is invited to present a seminar on senior management and then to run workshops for staff.

Government

The new government has adopted a 'tough on drugs' stance. Members of the Department of Education and Children's Services have been told by their political masters to work out what needs to be done in schools. Those who have received these instructions are not really on top of the issues and certainly do not know the latest research. They commission Jeanette to do a literature review for them which includes the 'grey literature' – that is, the reports and curriculum documents that have been developed and any evaluations of drug education programmes. Her time lines are very tight, as it has to be done 'yesterday'.

Education and training activities

Formal education and training of their members is likely to be a responsibility of several stakeholder groups. Whilst some will do it in-house, others will make provision through an assortment of partnership arrangements with universities and similar bodies. They may want you to be involved in the following ways by:

- Contributing expertise and perhaps writing material for their professional courses.
- Providing formal accreditation for their courses.

- Offering university programmes (short courses, diplomas, degree or postgraduate courses such as master's or 'professional doctorates') tailored to their needs in some way.
- Acting as an examiner for their professional exams.

Stakeholders may also be prepared to contribute to your teaching programmes, perhaps by:

- Offering lectures.
- Sitting on advisory panels.
- Assisting as examiners.
- Helping to formulate courses.

Here are some examples of the sorts of things that this work might involve.

Professional associations and unions

The national umbrella organisation for trade unions is concerned about falling membership levels and wants to start a major initiative to recruit new members. It appreciates that local union organisers may need to be trained to do this work. It approaches the employment studies unit of a major university and asks it to develop a range of distance training materials for distribution to local officials. The university accepts this offer and persuades the stakeholder to let the university run the programme and award a certificate to those who successfully complete it.

NGOs

A large US NGO that focuses on assisting poorer countries to develop their local economic infrastructure is concerned that its staff have insufficient expertise in economics, business and management. It therefore contacts the economics department of a major university and asks for some sort of training. The university agrees to stage a series of intensive short courses in development economics. Contact with the organisation and the students proves to be a useful network-building exercise for the researchers in the department.

Business

A large multinational corporation has just arrived in Botswana to set up a brewery. The managers know little about local employment laws. They approach the law lecturers at the university, who are happy to provide a diploma course for both managers from overseas and local senior staff.

Government

The senior staff in the department of social services are concerned about the difficulties experienced by social workers in dealing with their 'clients'. The social workers tell them that they feel stressed, stretched and also ill prepared to deal with the conflict that often arises between themselves and their 'clients', let alone with helping them to manage the conflicts in their own lives. Senior staff decide that a training programme is in order and approach the local university's department of social work and social policy to provide some weekend workshops on conflict, anger and stress management. The demand is so great that the university sets up a diploma course directed towards people in the helping professions. It invites senior staff in the department of social services to sit on the programme's advisory committee.

Participation in your stakeholders' governance

Many stakeholders want to involve people from outside their organisation in their governing bodies. This widens the basis of their expertise and provides a range of points of view. It may also add status and authority. University staff are among the outsiders they like to have involved. They might invite you to be:

- A non-executive director.
- On their executive bodies.
- On their sub-committees, especially the ones dealing with policy or development.

Here are some examples of how you might get involved.

Professional associations and unions

A large car workers' union was anxious to develop strategies for future development, especially in a climate of globalisation of the industry. It approached Darrel, a sociology professor who specialised in the study of the industry, and asked him to join the union's strategy working party.

NGOs

A small charity providing outreach support to street sex workers was growing fast but lacked expertise in the complex issues surrounding moving its clients on and out of prostitution. It asked Cindy, a senior academic in the social policy department of its local university, to join the management team of the charity as a volunteer in order to contribute her expertise. Cindy had an interest in the subject and was able to integrate her work with the charity into her research work.

Business

Luigi was conducting research on how companies hold their annual general meetings. As a result of his fieldwork he became well known in this field. A local but substantial company asked Luigi to join its board of directors so that he could contribute his expertise on communication with shareholders.

Government

Peter was an academic lawyer and an expert in social security matters. The government had a standing committee that was responsible for reviewing the operation of the law in this area. Peter was asked to chair the committee and produce an annual report for the Minister.

Involvement in your stakeholders' on-going activities

Outside input into their activities is crucial for stakeholder groups. There are many occasions and circumstances when this will be required and it will take various forms. You might be asked to:

- Be on their working parties or committees.
- Provide feedback on various sorts of documents.
- Consult on particular policies, programmes or practices.

Here are some examples of this type of activity. Our example is of just one man – Steve, a social anthropologist specialising in a remote South American country. When that country experienced a large amount of civil unrest the complete gamut of national and international stakeholders flocked to his door for assistance.

Professional associations and unions

Much of the civil unrest was associated with economic instability, high unemployment and inflation. Steve was contacted by an international congress of trade unions and asked for a briefing on the situation, as they were concerned about the plight of workers in the country.

NGOs

A charity with a large number of projects in the region asked Steve to come to an emergency meeting to discuss the likely prospects of stability in the country, as it needed to know whether it had to pull its workers out.

Business

The Corned Beef Company had major business interests in the same South American country and also contacted Steve, asking him to give it an emergency briefing on the impact that the civil unrest was likely to have on economic stability and the risks associated with its investments.

Government

Some academics on a field trip to the country were taken hostage by the rebels. The Foreign Ministry of Steve's home government contacted him urgently and asked him to join the team negotiating with the rebels.

In this chapter we have discussed likely stakeholders in some depth and considered some of the ways in which you might work with them. In the next chapter we deal with how you might go about this work.

6   How to Network with your Stakeholders

This chapter explains the ways that you might go about networking with your stakeholder networks, and offers some tips on how to begin, the things to do and the things to avoid.

How do you get to do this stuff?

You will normally be invited to do such activities or win the bids for them if some or all of the following things apply to you:

- You have got to know relevant people, developed sound relations with them and have reached an appreciation of their needs.
- Your work is in circulation in the public sphere and it is known to be what the stakeholder wants.
- You regularly appear in the press or in the publications read by your stakeholders.
- You lead a high-profile working life and are frequently seen doing excellent work in the places that matter.
- You get a good reputation for making an important contribution among the right people in the right circles.
- You belong to the groups who get to hear about such opportunities.
- You have influential friends and colleagues who put your name forward when names are needed.
- People are aware of your interests and availability.
- You respect those you work with as equal partners.
- You put together impressive tenders/winning bids.

Your value to stakeholders is in your special skills and expertise, and you need to keep these finely tuned. Stakeholders will not usually need you if you simply replicate what they have already – they want you to enhance what they have in some way or another.

Of course, particular stakeholder work will require particular sets of skills. For instance, you will probably be invited to prepare discussion documents or papers on particular issues if you are recognised as someone who is able to:

- Use their knowledge of the field and their networks to identify trends and patterns.
- Distil issues down to their essence, or 'cut through the crap' (as they say in less polite circles).
- Put new issues on the agenda.
- Provide a balanced but incisive report.
- Write in a style free from jargon and make your work accessible to non-academic readers.
- Deliver written work to deadlines and in good shape.

In sum, once you are well known in your space, invitations to do these sorts of activities will probably flow in quite regularly. But, if you hide your light under a bushel, this work will not normally come your way even if you are pretty good at what you do inside the university.

What if my stakeholders don't know me yet?

If stakeholders are to know that you exist, you have to do profile work and network in the places and circles where you want to be seen and known. And you will have to accept that it takes a while for visibility to translate into interest, acceptance, rapport, trust and reputation and then into invitations and successful tenders. Your early profile work might include such things as:

- Volunteering your services.
- Asking people for introductions.
- Contacting the press about your work.
- Placing articles in the right publications.
- Going to the 'right' events.
- Engineering invitations to the functions attended by the people you want to know.
- Arranging meetings with key contact people to discuss your work and how it links with their interests. Remember that first impressions often last, so keep the tips in Table 2 in mind.

TABLE 2 Do's and don'ts of stakeholder visits to your university

Do	Don't
Arrange a decent room and be free of interruptions	Meet them in your office and then take phone calls or answer students' knocks at the door while they are sitting there
Allocate sufficient but not excessive time	Make them wait and then squeeze them in for ten minutes between a lecture and tutorial
Make sure all equipment is working and have your materials and displays ready	Have them hanging about while the technician is called to fix the equipment and then when it is finally ready present them with half-baked ideas
Serve good coffee and tasty morsels	Take them to the canteen and let them buy their own coffee
Have some good-quality materials for them to take away	Let them leave empty-handed
Follow up immediately	Leave it to them to follow up or let so much time elapse that they have forgotten who you are when you finally call

Here are some of the techniques used by people to build their profile with stakeholders.

Bill's research expertise is in criminology and he is also involved in an ex-prisoner support and lobby group. He has devised a media strategy to gain public profile for the cause and for his work. He regularly puts out press releases on his latest papers. Indeed, if he is giving a paper at a conference he sends out the press releases two days before and includes his contact details. Usually these result in lots of media follow-up. The conference organisers don't mind, as it gives the conference publicity. However, they do get a bit upset if he spends most of his time at the conference giving interviews to the press rather than mixing with those who want to meet him.

Erin works in a medical health faculty. She has moved quite frequently to new academic posts in new cities. She has devised an entry strategy that allows her to quickly connect with her new sets of local stakeholders. When she arrives she finds out who the key players are, contacts them and arranges to meet at their workplaces. Her conversations with them demonstrate her interest and expertise in their fields and her value to them. She points out that she would be willing to sit on pertinent committees and to run workshops. Within the first few months she has usually presented workshops to the range of groups she needs to know. As they are seen to meet the stakeholders' needs there is inevitably lots of follow-up.

Paul works in a business school which provides plenty of short courses to cohorts of students from the large businesses that surround his campus. Paul starts to teach some of these students, thereby gaining knowledge of the businesses and what they need. He then visits the students at their place of work and they, as courtesy dictates, introduce him to their bosses. As a consequence, Paul has a legitimate opportunity to discuss with these senior managers what else he might provide for the firm. Because Paul's students really rate him – and tell their bosses that – he has a receptive audience.

Insider knowledge from the outside

Each stakeholder organisation will have its own culture and practices. These will impact on the ways in which stakeholders respond to you as a potential network partner. As such, it is absolutely imperative that you understand who you are dealing with. This can be quite a complex task. Getting to know individuals in the organisations is one way, watching them work and being a keen observer is another. A further way is to talk to people who are outside the culture but who know it well. These people will often be able to point to the blind spots of the insiders and also to the roadblocks you may confront in trying to get inside. Both insider knowledge and outsider knowledge are therefore essential to understanding how stakeholder organisations tick.

We can't cover the gamut of organisational cultures that you are likely to encounter among stakeholders. But, using the example of business, we offer some quick tips below on how you might resonate with such cultures. For more on this subject, we suggest that you read Schumacher's work, which is cited in the Further Reading suggestions at the end of this book.

- Learn what their needs are. Businesses are interested only in their own needs, not yours, and will fund only those things they see as meeting their needs. This means that you have to learn what their needs are and then represent them to the organisation in a way that also aligns them with your own.
- Make it clear in what ways you are a trained expert whose expertise is of direct and practical relevance to them. Show how you do/will meet their needs.
- Show that you also provide access to other expertise that is of value to them. For instance, potential employees are important to industry, and so you might bring with you your best and brightest graduate students.
- Winning work from industry may require you to make a presentation. And as Schumacher (*Get Funded!*, p. 129), says, 'pay close attention to the mode of delivery in the business world: slick, snappy and entertaining'. This means that, for once only, you can have a dispensation from our injunction not to use PowerPoint.
- Make it clear how you 'add value' to the organisation. You may be able to suggest some appealing new directions it had not thought of.
- You may choose to host an industry visit to the university. Make sure this is well prepared and that those visiting are treated as significant and respected guests.

What to do or not to do

We are going to return now to the five principal ways in which stakeholders might want to work with you that we identified earlier:

- Research, consultancy and evaluation projects.
- Professional development activities.
- Education and training activities.

- Participation in their governance.
- Involvement in their on-going activities.

We discuss some of the major do's and don'ts associated with each type of work in turn.

Research, consultancy or evaluation projects

In *Winning and Managing Research Funding* there is much information about stakeholder-funded research, consultancy or evaluation projects. We don't go into this again here, but would emphasise that you must have a good sense of the rules of each game. If you don't like the rules, don't play the game. Like contract research, consultancies and evaluations are very much on the stakeholder's terms and offer few opportunities for you to do your own thing. As in all academic work, however, you have a responsibility to pursue the work without fear or favour and to produce reports that are transparent (to make clear your methods and how you reached your conclusions) and robust.

Stakeholders may be anxious to achieve a particular result and may, as a consequence, try to steer you in certain directions. This can become especially fraught if your work gets caught up in internal political manoeuvring. At the same time, you may have some strong personal views. Despite all this, you must remain true to the best principles of research. Within the conventions of the consultancy or evaluation methodology that you are employing, your work must be able to be defended as robust on the following grounds. It must:

- Be recognised as a credible depiction of the situation by those well placed to know.
- Be 'at the highest level of achievable quality, methodological, theoretical and textual' as Paul Willis says in *The Ethnographic Imagination*.
- Provide a sufficient basis for others to build from in subsequent research or practical action.

It should be up to you who you choose to consult or provide evaluations for and with regard to what issues. Don't do it if:

- You cannot agree to the terms of reference.
- The amount of money is insufficient to cover the time involved or the costs.

- You have a major ideological disagreement with the stakeholder.
- You have a conflict of interest.
- You do not really have the expertise or the time.
- You are not willing to be honest with your stakeholders; in other words, if you are not prepared to provide a 'warts and all' report.

Professional development activities

Invitations may come from groups that are very experienced at bringing in outside people or from those who do not have a clue how best to do it. Whatever the case, you need to be clear about the following matters.

Dates and times

Are these firmly fixed or can they be negotiated to fit round your other commitments?

Place and travel

Is the venue easy for you to get to or is it an out-of-the-way place that will involve lots of time to get there, possibly involving time-consuming stopovers, for instance?

Expenses

Are they all covered? You will need to be specific about such matters as: travel (including taxis where necessary, tickets that enable you to rearrange your schedule and matters such as whether you can travel any way other than economy class); accommodation (including location, quality and the facilities available to support your work); *per diem* expenses if necessary to cover incidental costs whilst you are there; and preliminary expenses such as printing and copying.

A fee for you

Most stakeholders will expect to pay for your services. Local arrangements for academics vary somewhat. Your university may allow you to keep the fee yourself (provided that you don't spend too many days a year doing such work) or may split it with you (allowing you to have part of it paid as salary or to keep it for research funds) or it may want to keep it all (although this is rare, as it deters academics from doing such work).

The level at which the fee should be set can be difficult to gauge, though there may be guidelines from your university, union or association. It might be based on your salary (as a minimum threshold) or be set by what the 'market' will bear (as an upper threshold). The fee should be in proportion to the amount of time that the event or activity takes you away from your university work. If you are in doubt about what to ask for or negotiate about, ask your department head or research centre director. If you do have to share your fee with the university, or want to, then make sure that you ask for enough to leave you with a worthwhile amount – bearing in mind that the work may have other, non-financial beneficial spin-offs for you. You should negotiate with the stakeholder about payment not only for the event itself but also for your preparation and travel time. Don't be shy about asking for a fair amount. Don't be greedy, but don't be too cost-humble either. You should be aware that some stakeholders can and do pay huge fees to certain snake-oil merchants who operate on the KISS principle (Keep It Simple, Stupid).

Venue

Does the venue where you will be working have facilities for copying and printing and other resources necessary for you as a speaker? If you will be using technology such as PowerPoint, will it all work for you on the day and be compatible with what you bring along? Is the venue near your accommodation and will you need a map or transport to help you get between the two? Make sure that you have contingency arrangements to cope with the inevitable snarl-ups that will happen – for instance, make sure that you have the mobile (cell) phone number of the organisers and that they have yours. Even if you will be collected and ferried around, make sure that you have the details of where you are supposed to be going and when. When it comes to the room itself, clarify what it is like and whether you can rearrange the furniture.

Their expectations of you

Make sure that you clarify well ahead of time exactly what the stakeholders expect you to do. They may want you just to do your 'spot' or they may want written materials too or copies of your presentation. You need to know what format the session will take and how you are expected to handle the time.

Audience

Get accurate information on your audience. This includes who they are, what they expect to get out of the sessions, how they have been briefed and so on. This will enable you to prepare more effectively.

Time-lines

Agree a clear timetable with the stakeholders with regard to things that they may need in advance. They will usually want a short CV, an abstract of what you will do and perhaps even a picture of you for their flyers/brochures.

Translation

If there are language issues involved with regard to the event itself, you need to sort out well in advance what kind of arrangements will be made. If there is to be a translator, will they need to have an advance copy of your presentation? If the event is to be 'Signed' for people with hearing difficulties, make sure that you are briefed on the best way of working with the signer.

Dress

Find out how formal the event will be and whether you will be expected to do things such as attend formal dinners. Take the right clothes for any activities and the weather.

Permanent records

Do your stakeholders propose to have the session video-taped or audio-taped? If so, make sure that you are content with this and how they plan to use the recording.

Undertaking professional development activities puts you under the spotlight. How well you do them will influence your chances of getting further invitations, not to mention your capacity to have an impact in your area and with your chosen stakeholders. So make sure you do it right.

You are also entitled to have expectations of the stakeholder. Here is a list of things that you should make sure of.

- Ensure that everything to do with all the matters we discussed above comes to you in writing and in plenty of time. Insist on full details of travel arrangements, especially if you are in a country in which you do not speak the language. If they want you, they have to make it easy for you to do your work. Do not consent to being treated like a second-class citizen, but don't be a prima donna either.
- Agree with your stakeholders how you will be introduced and represented to the participants. Make sure that any information they have (from your website or CV and so on) is accurate and up to date and that they use it properly and appropriately. To do this, you will need to establish an effective working relationship with the organisers. Such introductions are part of developing your profile.
- Make sure that your itinerary suits you. You will need time to relax or perhaps to meet people who can help you with your work. Ensure that proper arrangements are made to properly 'host' you so that you are not left floundering around in an unfamiliar social environment.
- Be certain about the payment methods for both your fee and your expenses. It is not usually a good idea to pay your own plane fare and then reclaim it, as that might involve you in a lengthy wait before you can pay your credit card bill.

- If the session is to be evaluated by the participants then ask for copies of the report. Otherwise, ensure they provide you with informal feedback so that you can improve for next time.

Some handy hints on doing professional development

1. Never accept an invitation on the spot. Always ask for the details and indicate that you will need time to think about it.
2. To mitigate against disasters such as lost luggage or theft, always have spare copies of the papers or disks you will need to use, perhaps in different bags.
3. Always keep a folder with all the details of the event, addresses, contact names, etc., on you. Do not leave home without it. Don't be over-reliant on a single electronic device such as a handheld computer.
4. Give yourself plenty of time. You don't want to arrive all breathless and flustered, and you do want to check out the room and the equipment beforehand.
5. Make a point of mingling with people and stay a while if you can. Don't be a fly-in, fly-out prima donna or one of those people who escape as soon as they have delivered their pearls of wisdom. This smacks of arrogance and points to lack of interest in the people in your stakeholder group. Bad impressions often last longer than good ones.
6. When you leave, don't slink out the door. Make a point of speaking to your hosts to thank them for the invitation. Talk positively about the event (remember, they will have put a lot of work into its organisation) and indicate your willingness to participate in future activities.
7. Do not give away the copyright of any papers that you have distributed and also ensure that all the material they take of yours is identifiable as such. Make clear to the stakeholders that they must ask your permission to use your material again. Do not let them have copies of your notes, even though many will press you for them. You may be able to make sense of them, but others may not be able to.
8. Don't let people press you into doing extra work after the event that was not agreed and paid for unless you can foresee non-financial benefits in such a goodwill gesture.

Hopefully, if you follow the above suggestions you will be successful in managing scenarios like those in the following stories.

Chris was sitting in his office marking papers when he got a phone call from the president of the local Rotary club, who seemed agitated. The caller demanded, 'Where are you? Why aren't you here? The meeting is due to start in an hour!' Chris had no idea what he was talking about.

An explanation finally emerged. During the previous semester Chris had had an informal chat with the president, who had casually invited him to come and give an address at the annual Rotary conference. There had been no communication after that as far as Chris knew, so he had assumed that the Rotary had decided not to follow though. The president assured him that a fax had been sent with the details on it; Chris had not received it.

The president tried to press Chris to drop everything, rush to the conference and give an off-the-cuff address. Chris was unwilling and unable to do so. He never gives unprepared talks because he knows that he is not good at them. Nor did he have a suitable talk on file that he could use for the occasion. So he refused, explaining that the fax had not arrived and that he was unprepared.

The president was furious. While he was willing to acknowledge that Rotary should have made personal contact with Chris rather than just relying on the fax, he could not understand that an expert could not just talk of the cuff. In the end Chris did not go and his relationship with Rotary has been frosty ever since.

Lesley spends her academic life rushing between commitments. While she is brilliant in her field and in great demand by her stakeholders, she is very disorganised in the ways she runs her affairs. She was due to give an address at a professional organisation's international conference, but five days before her departure date she found that she did not have a visa to get into the country. Luckily she was able to pull some strings and get one quickly to enable her to leave only a day late. Fortunately too the conference organisers were able to shift her opening keynote address to the final day of the conference. On arrival at her destination she found that she did not have all the details of her hotel and the conference venue with her. She had to call home at midnight local time and talk her rather aggrieved partner through the mess on her desk to find them.

Education and training activities

There are two main ways of providing education and training to stakeholders: either you become involved in their activities or they use your university as a provider to them. Each has its own requirements and complexities.

If you are involved in their training courses, this is likely to be a well structured activity very much under the stakeholder's control. As with many other things, they will know exactly what they want and will expect you to 'deliver'. You may, for instance, be involved in giving training to trainee professionals such as lawyers or accountants. The variety of possibilities here is endless. If your stakeholders decide to access your university to provide their members with education and training the university will obviously have a much greater degree of control over the process.

As with other sorts of stakeholder work (and especially professional development work), make sure that everything is agreed and confirmed between the partners and is fair to all sides. You must be:

• Absolutely clear about their expectations.
• Absolutely clear about which of these you can meet.
• In what ways.
• At what costs to you and thus to them.

If the education and/or training is to be provided through the university, make sure that your stakeholder understands the ways in which your institution operates with regard to teaching. Keep in mind that what may be common sense to you as a university teacher may not be at all clear to stakeholders. Much detail will have to be both negotiated and then spelt out in writing. This will include:

• Prerequisites and exemptions.
• Enrolment processes, fees and charges.
• The length and composition of the programme.
• Work experience or field placement requirements.
• Mode and site of delivery (face-to-face, on-line, on or off campus).
• Expectations of students with regard to attendance, participation, work load, assessment types and processes.
• Standards of work required.

- Access to university facilities such as the libraries.
- Student appeal procedures.
- Final awards.
- Regular processes of programme evaluation, review and revision.
- Membership of programme committees.

Things to avoid in the negotiation stage include:

- 'Special deals' that compromise quality just to get the contract.
- Seeking *post hoc* support from your university.
- Being passive. Stakeholders may think they know what they want but they may not know what else is available or possible. Take the chance to open up new options for them.
- Promising more than you can deliver.

Once agreements are reached, do not:

- Fail to honour the deal in any way.
- Start excluding the stakeholder from the processes.
- Drop any standard on the basis of special pleading, for instance by letting students proceed without the prerequisites or by constantly giving exemptions. Remember that they are enrolled in a university and are gaining a university qualification. So there should be no compromise on standards. If a programme bears a university badge it must be a standard bearer of university-level education.

At all times, after such matters are settled, the lines of communication between you, the stakeholder and the rest of the university need to be kept open.

Max was teaching on a professional doctorate in health. This degree was offered, on a fee-paying basis, to local students and also to a select group of students situated in another country. Max was disappointed to find that an assignment by one of the latter students bore no relation to the topic. It was simply a report the student had written for a government committee. He naturally failed the student's assignment and let the programme director know. The director ▶

▶ suggested that he might like to reconsider, given that the student had been instrumental in securing the enrolment of the cohort of foreign students, resulting in a handsome cash inflow for the university. Max gleaned from his conversation with the director that this student had been told that his doctorate could largely be gained on the basis of the reports he had already written before being enrolled in the programme. Max refused to pass the student and indicated in writing that he was most concerned about the ethics of the programme.

Involvement in your stakeholders' governance

Whilst being involved in the governance arrangements of stakeholders may bring many networking benefits, it can be quite onerous and time-consuming. You may have to sit through a lot of meetings, for example, that are of little interest or value to you.

In taking on such a position you should clarify your role's obligations and responsibilities. You need to be clear about such things as:

- The number and duration of meetings and the likely amount of normal business.
- Any likely additional responsibilities.
- The duration of your appointment and options for reappointment.

You might ask to see the previous year's minutes so that you can assess how relevant your expertise and experience are. This will also allow you to see how potentially useful the appointment is to your other work. If either is tangential then don't accept the position – it will be a burden and your reputation will suffer if you are of no use to them.

Once you have accepted a post, you must take your responsibilities seriously, which means:

- Attending all the meetings (no constant apologies, late arrivals or early departures).
- Being well prepared for meetings by making sure you have read the agenda and all the attached papers.
- Having some views on the issues raised rather than sitting there with nothing to contribute.

- Having some self-control over your use of linguistic space; in other words, do not hog the time.
- Contributing on the basis of your expertise and on other matters of more general interest.
- Volunteering for the occasional working party or sub-committee (but not too many).

Nancy was known among her immediate colleagues as very ambitious and as someone who was constantly on the look-out for new experiences to include in her CV. She was also quite a high-flyer in her field and well known in government circles. She accepted all the invitations but rarely attended the meetings. When she did, she was unprepared and her contributions were unhelpful, to say the least. While she still looked sufficiently good on paper to eventually secure a senior university management post in another country, she had a lasting poor reputation in her home state.

Involvement in your stakeholders' on-going activities

Academics often do occasional work for their stakeholders. It might involve informal and unpaid work such as feedback on draft documents or policies. Academics who do this sort of voluntary work often see it as a community service, a gesture of goodwill or as one way to build their networks and reputation. Such work may also be undertaken under contract. If the work you are doing is in this category you need to go to *Winning and Managing Research Funding* and read what it says about contracts. But what if you are volunteering your services?

We think it is worth insisting that a gift economy can still exist even in our 'user pays' world and we would not quarrel with your good intentions. However, it is worth considering to whom you might best offer your gifts. We think it is fine if, in moderation, you volunteer your services to those who cannot afford them or if you do the odd freebie as a 'loss leader'. This is provided you can reasonably find the time and if it does not distract or detract too much from your other activities. However, we know a number of very busy academics who do such unpaid work at the drop of a hat for stakeholders with plenty of loot. Perhaps they:

- Hope that it will eventually pay off in the form of research, evaluation or consultancy contracts.
- Are so flattered to be asked that they would not dream of charging.
- Do not know how to say no to powerful bodies.
- Do not know how to ask for payment.

We have also often seen such people passed over for contracts by others who charge like wounded bulls. If your stakeholders have reasonable amounts of money at their disposal, it is reasonable for them to pay you. Ask for advice at your university if you are unsure how much to charge. You should not provide such bodies with free services too often or for too long.

In this chapter we have looked at the practicalities of working with stakeholders in a variety of ways. This can be exhausting and complicated work and we would urge you to be quite controlled about what you take on and why. In the next chapter we deal with using dissemination networks.

7 Dissemination Networks

In this chapter we explain what we mean by dissemination, identify the main dissemination networks that are of concern to you and then focus on media dissemination networks.

Dissemination – what does it mean?

Dissemination means different things to the many different people and groups associated with universities. For individual universities, dissemination is associated with marketing the quality of the institution and thus enhancing its drawing power. It is about getting a reputation for teaching and research achievement that will bring in students, money and prestige. For your faculty or research group, dissemination is largely similar.

The stuff they do not want to 'get out' is called:

- Lies.
- Media distortion.
- Misrepresentation.
- Idle gossip.
- Bad publicity.
- Mismanagement by the PR staff, who, incidentally, have just lost their jobs!

For governments and 'knowledge managers', dissemination is associated with 'impact', which, in their view, can and must be monitored, measured and, where appropriate, rewarded financially. It's worth noting that counting dissemination and impact has become something of a fool's errand on the part of governments. Assessing 'impact' is very labour-intensive, potentially costly and notoriously difficult. The methods of counting involved are invariably methodologically flawed and the whole emphasis on output and impact often results in a 'quantity over quality' mentality. It thus skews the whole academic enterprise in the wrong direction. Clearly dissemination is important, but not in the ways conceived of by the bean counters.

What do you want, really really want?

For an individual academic, dissemination is about getting your work, ideas and name out and about in the right places, among the right people and in the right ways. These people will usually include current and potential students, academics in your field, people in your stakeholder groups and more broadly the public. The places will include whatever academic journal and books these people are likely to read and whatever teaching and research venues they are in. You will also be pleased to achieve some media coverage of your work – provided it is reasonably accurate and positive. This is because you know that research and teaching are of interest to sections of the public and that they will want to hear about it. Most academics are not interested in fame for its own sake. Well, only a bit.

You may want any or all of the following:

- To be well known inside your field.
- Students flocking to your courses because you are acknowledged as a great teacher.
- Graduate students clamouring for you to supervise them, so you can pick those you really want to work with.
- To be in print in good journals and books.
- To be widely read and widely and favourably cited.
- To be respected and in demand among your stakeholders.
- Positive media coverage.

Overall you want to be a knowledgeable and skilled communicator who is able to achieve all the above with ease and panache. You want to be able to speak to various audiences well and in the right voice.

Not all publicity is good publicity. You don't want to be well known for such things as being:

- Pedantic and ponderous at conferences.
- The dreariest teacher in the history department.

- Crucified on talk-back radio.
- Publishing drivel.

So what are dissemination networks?

Simply, these are the networks that enable you to get what you really really want. There are three main types.

Academic dissemination networks

Much of what you need to know about these is in Chapter 3 and in *Writing for Publication* and *Teaching and Supervision*. Important nodes in these networks are:

- Academic journal editors and editorial teams.
- Editors of book series.
- Commissioning editors from publishing houses.
- Conference and special interest group (SIG) organisers.
- Research and teaching leaders in universities.
- Academics who peer-review for journals.
- Academics in key positions on, or who review for, research funding bodies.
- Academics who occupy key positions in funding councils.
- Academics who are understood as leaders in their fields.
- Student group leaders, and editors and writers of student publications.

Stakeholder dissemination networks

Chapter 4 contains what you need to know about these. Important nodes may be individuals or organisations and include:

- Editors of professional journals and newsletters.
- People in leadership roles in individual or umbrella organisations, for example their presidents, chief executives or general secretaries.
- People in key posts in individual and umbrella organisations such as heads of departments or people with particular responsibilities relevant to you.

- Civil servants and policy makers with responsibilities relevant to your work.
- Politicians.
- Office bearers and workers in relevant non-governmental organisations.

Media dissemination networks

In what remains of this chapter we will focus on these. They include not only print and broadcast media but also Web-based media (such as on-line newspapers and websites associated with radio and television programmes) and also alternative Web-based media outlets, which have sprung up largely in opposition to mainstream media and politics. The main nodes in these networks are:

- Journalists (staffers, freelance and those who are commissioned).
- Editors or their equivalent in Web-based media (particularly those responsible for special segments of their newspaper or programme, for instance the sport or food editors).
- Researchers for radio and television programmes.
- Media liaison people in your university (PR, marketing, press officers).

Media links and logics

We think that academics need to develop some understanding of how various aspects of the media work and should consider how best to share their ideas with the press. Fox and Levin, whose book *How to Work with the Media* is listed in our Further Reading offer suggestions that are very helpful in this regard.

Media profile

There are two ways to look at this: having a media profile and having the media profile your work.

To have a media profile means that you appear regularly in the press over an extended period and have become known to the press and the public. Usually it is because of your expertise in your particular field. This means that, when media commentary is wanted, yours is among the first names that spring to the mind of journalists.

It also means that the public will often associate the particular issue with your ideas. Some academics have such a media profile and have, for instance, come to host their own TV shows or radio programmes or have their own regular newspaper columns. They have become academic celebrities. You will, undoubtedly, know examples pertinent to your own country.

Of course, some academics have developed a media profile because they are involved in controversial research and have become part of a media war among academics or between academics and their university. They may lose their profile once public interest in the particular issue dies down. Others may have a media profile for all the wrong reasons. They may, for instance, have been caught plagiarising others' work, falsifying results, or 'soft marking' and have thus become the focus of critical media attention.

If the media profile your work, it means that your work is out in the public sphere along with your name. However, the ideas are likely to have a higher profile than you. You might for instance be part of a media debate on a particular topic and your research may be drawn upon in the coverage along with that of others. Of course, if the media constantly profile your ideas then you may well develop a media profile.

Most academics fit into this latter category. Most of you will not become academic celebrities, although you may indeed have a period of time in your academic career when your work attracts media coverage for a while. The rest of this chapter is mainly concerned with helping you to ensure that the media profile your work in ways that you feel comfortable about.

What's in it for you?

We have discuss the benefits of media dissemination of your work in *Building an Academic Career*. To summarise briefly, it is worth developing media dissemination networks because media coverage of your ideas provides you with the opportunity to:

- Educate the general public or your particular publics.
- Participate in public debate.
- Influence policy and practice.
- Be seen by the bean counters as fulfilling your obligation to have an impact.
- Enhance your status within your university and among your stakeholders.

- Acquire additional academic opportunities.
- Gain some coverage, which often leads to more coverage.
- Draw attention to work that your stakeholder may have tried to bury.

Patricia and Dale had done some work for the Canadian government on the impact of taxation on poverty. They returned their report to the government department on time and waited for it to be released. They waited, and waited, and waited. Eventually they became impatient and started writing to and calling the Ministry. They were assured that the report would be released in due course. In fact, on Christmas Eve the report was released on the Web, and only on the Web. Patricia and Dale decided that they would adopt two dissemination strategies: to give lots of conference papers at conferences normally attended by journalists, and to issue a press release drawing attention to their report. The press and other news media picked up the story and ran it for several days. The *coup de grâce* came when Dale was invited to appear on a major national talk show.

But it's no picnic

Having the media profile your ideas is, however, no picnic, and the disadvantages of working with the media include:

- Your inability to control what is said about you and your work.
- The excessive time it can involve.
- The disruption it can cause to your normal work patterns.
- Misrepresentation of you and your ideas.
- The usual lack of an equally visible right of reply.
- Public harassment.

Madeleine is an academic with expertise in psychiatry. She has been involved in assessing the impact of the incarceration of refugees on the mental health of children in refugee camps in Australia. She is shocked at the harm to children she has found and along with her

▶

professional association has participated in media campaigns to promote the rights of refugees and the removal of children from the camps. She has received threatening phone calls and hate email, and the more visible she has become the more such mail has grown in volume and vehemence.

When the media contact you

Usually the media will want you to provide background or some quotes or an interview for a newspaper story or for the news on radio or TV. They may also want you to do radio talk back or to be part of a discussion panel on radio or TV.

If you have a media profile or are well known in your field by your academic peers or stakeholders the press may contact you to comment on a particular story they are pursuing. If you don't have a media profile your name will most likely have arisen from their conversations with others in your field. They may have little idea of who you are or where you are coming from. Or they may have the wrong idea. Often they are trying to provide what they call 'balance', or two sides of a story, and you may have been identified by your peers as someone who sits on one side of the fence. Very often the fence is of their construction and they couch the story in simple binary terms. You may find that you have been painted into a corner you do not wish to occupy. The scenario may go something like this.

When things go wrong

You come into work to find that your voice mail has several messages from a journalist. They include her contact details and a brief indication of the story line she is following. She has also sent you several email messages and left messages for you with any other staff member she has been able to reach. She makes it sound urgent, asking you to get back to her as soon as you possibly can, but without telling you when she will be available. When you do finally manage to reach her you find that:

▶
- Her deadline is excruciatingly tight.
- She has already decided on the spin of the article.
- It is couched in binary or sensationalist terms.
- She has little knowledge of the topic but has a strong point of view.
- She wants to pick your brains about what you know.
- She wants to decide whether you and your opinions are newsworthy.

How do you, the media novice, usually respond when the media call?

- You get excited and wander the corridors looking for someone to tell that the press want to speak to *you*.
- You call back several times to find that the journalist is constantly on other calls or out of the office.
- The day ends and you leave your home number on her message bank and email.
- When she finally reaches you, you spend a good deal of time offering her the benefit of your expertise, explaining the complexities of the situation, referring her to other papers to read, and emailing her several of your own academic papers.
- You arrive early at the newsagent to collect a copy of the paper in which you expect to feature, only to find any one of the following possibilities. The article does not appear or is buried in the later pages. Perhaps you get a tiny mention towards the end of the article but with your academic title wrong. Perhaps you are misquoted or allocated a position in a debate which you do not hold. Perhaps you are made to look rather foolish or pompous. And so on and so forth.
- You contact the journalist but she does not take your calls or call back.
- You contact the editor to try to get a right of reply. He suggests that you write a letter to the editor.
- You resolve never to get sucked in again. Once bitten twice shy, you think.

But, the next time the press call, you perversely repeat the process.

We have all been there and done that. We could tell many similar stories involving radio and TV, but we won't because they expose yet further the naivety of novice academics trying to get their ideas out through the press. Clearly things can go wrong and you need to be alert to the dangers. But this is only one possible scenario – not all journalists are like the one above, you can learn how to make the best of such opportunities and also to take some initiative.

When you contact the media

Some academics are very proactive. They take the initiative and do the following sorts of things:

- Contact the university press office with their latest news – a new research grant for example – and have the press office develop a press release for circulation.
- Contact journalists and indicate their availability on certain issues.
- When a particular topic is dominating the media they contact the editors and suggest a new angle.
- Write opinion pieces and articles about their research for the newspaper.
- Make calls to talk-back radio shows and offer their opinion.
- Ensure that information about any conferences or seminars they conduct is provided to the press. Some conference organisers use media liaison people to assist them to promote the conference and its main speakers.
- Take advantage of media coverage of conferences and introduce themselves to the journalists.

Other academics are less proactive but are sensitive to media possibilities. They do such things as:

- Leave a statement of their expertise with the university press office – just in case!
- Ensure that they feature in the regular university newsletters, knowing that the mainstream media sometimes pick stories up from them.
- Couch their conference paper titles and abstracts in ways that may entice media interest.
- If something particularly pertinent to their work comes up in the news, they behave more proactively for a while.

Jean-Paul worked in a particularly controversial and sensitive area. Generally he did not spend significant effort on getting his work into the media – partly because he did not want to become the focus of media attention. However, when the government decided to pass punitive legislation directly about his area of expertise, he decided, with his vice-chancellor, that he should contribute to the public debate. He drafted a press statement in consultation with his university's press officer and contacted some journalists he knew to be sympathetic to his point of view. He also wrote a feature article for a major French newspaper. As a result, he was asked to appear on television and radio programmes, both as a commentator in current affairs programming and in talk-back programmes. Although the media campaign that he was part of did not change the legislation, it did seem to have quite an impact on public opinion.

As this vignette indicates, sometimes working with the media can pay off in terms of media profile and coverage. The most common scenario is for this to be short-lived and followed by nothing at all until the next media opportunity arises.

However, sometimes attempts to get things into the media don't pay off and press releases are met with deathly silence. Why the deathly silence? It might happen because the news they want to convey is not considered newsworthy by the press.

What is newsworthy?

According to Bivins' *Handbook for Public Relations*, in our list of Further Reading, for something to be considered newsworthy to the media it must have most of the following features. In considering your work you should be able to answer the following questions with regard to each feature.

- Consequence. Will it be regarded as important to the reader or audience?
- Interest. Is it entertaining, unusual, controversial, exciting?
- Timeliness. Is it current, or a new angle on an old problem?

- Proximity. Can people connect with the ideas? Does it hit home, resonate?
- Prominence. Does it connect with prominent people, or institutions?

Additionally, the media particularly enjoy a good bunfight.

For years John, a grammarian, had been sending pieces to newspapers, magazines and radio and TV presenters about his work on the importance of punctuation. No-one had taken a blind bit of notice. Suddenly, when Lynne Truss's book *Eats, Shoots and Leaves* was published in 2003 and became a runaway bestseller, John found himself in huge demand to contribute reviews and other articles to the press and to take part in radio and television discussions about punctuation.

What kind of academics do the media really want?

According to media workers, academics are chosen for interviews because they are:

- Available when the media need them – a key element in managing the media successfully.
- Succinct.
- Relaxed.
- Reliable.
- Attractive.
- Able to translate professional language into something accessible to a particular media audience.
- Media-savvy.

But what kind of academics do the media really *really* want?

They want you to be all the above and preferably:

- Entertaining.
- Charismatic.
- Provocative.
- Controversial.

Many academics who shine in lectures and conferences may go to mush or suddenly speak gobbledygook when in front of a camera or microphone. Dealing with the media has not been part of most academics' professional or academic training and so it does not come 'naturally'. Any academic who wants to deal with the media successfully needs to ensure that they have been well trained in how to do so. Indeed, this has been included by the UK Economic and Social Research Council in its guidance about the preparation of research students for academic life.

Mediating the media

While we would strongly advise you to try to get some good training in how to handle the media, there are some pointers that we can offer here. Remember, however, that the media differ between countries and you need to check out what your local media culture and expectations are and adjust what you do accordingly.

First things first

If you want your work to gain media profile then you need to get the basics in place.

- *Understand what 'newsworthy' means* for the media and then apply the concept to your own work. Don't waste your own or others' time with stuff that is not newsworthy and can't be made to appear so.
- *Decide which media you want to target and do some research.* You need to have a sense of which outlets you can realistically expect to cover your work. Make sure you become familiar with them and their audiences. You need to know what is normally covered, how it is covered and who the usual journalists are. Keep in mind that it is important to get your name in newspapers because they are the prime source that other media use when preparing a story.
- *Develop a contact list.* This should include the journalists who tend to cover your field or who work for the outlets you wish to target. Highlight those whose reporting you like. You need to try to get to know these people and always have all their contact details to hand. More than that, it is worth cultivating particular

journalists you like and trust. Do them favours and they'll be more than ready to help you.

- *Find out what facilities are available in your university to assist you.* Most universities now have press officers and PR people (often trained journalists) who may help you in various ways. They may, for instance, write press releases about your work, provide you with their media contact lists, be prepared to provide media training to groups of staff or be able to provide you with media kits containing things like advice about how to write press releases.
- *Develop a short biographical statement and a longer media résumé.* Always have these on hand. Your short biographical statement should include the most basic details that you want the media to use in any coverage of your work. Your longer media résumé clarifies your expertise and experience. This can be given to your press officer, who will share it with the press when they contact her. Journalists often contact local universities looking for expert commentators on particular issues and they often go through the press office.
- *Practise new ways of talking and writing.* Media-savvy academics can demystify academic language and make difficult ideas accessible. They are able to speak to the specific audience of the media outlet they are using. In a sense you have to 'deskill and reskill' yourself to be able do this. Practise writing brochures, short articles or editorials for newsletters or for house and trade publications. These require a new sort of writing discipline.

Melissa worked in an area which, on the face of it, should have been very newsworthy. It was topical, controversial and cutting-edge – and included lots of human interest. But Melissa had great difficulty getting her stuff into the press, and on the one occasion she was on television she froze and was unable to speak without stuttering. Rather than just give up, Melissa went to see her institution's press officer, who organised a series of media training sessions for Melissa and other members of her department. These training sessions included some run by professional journalists from the print and broadcast media as well as some run by the press officer herself. In the course of the media training Melissa and her colleagues were:

▶ • Shown how to write press releases and given the opportunity to practise doing so.
- Interviewed for mock radio and television programmes and given the chance to critique their own and each other's performances.
- Helped to think about the do's and don'ts of successful media appearances.

Following this course, Melissa had much more success in getting her research disseminated in the media.

Now put your toe in the water

Even in the absence of a good media training course, like the one that Melissa's press officer organised, you can help yourself prepare for working with and disseminating your research through the media. In order to do so, you need to do several things, which we discuss below.

Learn to nutshell. This means identifying the kernel of what you want to say – your core message, if you like – and then identifying a few key points that you want to get across in relation to it.

- Do you have a hook? Can you spin? Have you got an angle? These are what grab people's attention.
- If you have any compelling human-interest narratives that bring your story alive, remind yourself of them. It's best if you can 'paint' some vivid pictures that bring your story to life for readers, listeners and/or viewers.
- Try to develop some catchy turns of phrase that the press may latch on to – yes, sound bites.
- Can you address the need-to-know factor? In other words, can you explain why the topic is of importance to the media audience?
- Can you succinctly but convincingly support your claims?
- Can you give examples?
- Can you make any suggestions for action?

Take some of your academic papers and try to do a nutshell for the press.

Rehearse. Try your media persona and style out on some friends who are not academics or with your university press officers or PR people. Are your ideas newsworthy? Are you able to get your complex ideas across succinctly and simply? Do you make sense to them? Are you engaging and interesting?

Try writing some media releases and backgrounders. Check how others do them. Share them with your press office or a friendly journalist and get feedback. Note that you must speak the language of the media you are dealing with and have a newsworthy topic and heading, supply information in descending order of importance and make available all contact details.

Start small. Gain your early experiences with local, lower-profile media that are not likely to be picked up by national or even international media. Your neighbourhood or university newspapers may be good places to start. As Fox and Levin who are listed in Further Reading, say, 'Talk to the local community before talking to the nation' (*How to Work the Media*, p. 12). However, be aware that the national press can pick up even low-profile media and you need to be cautious about what you do and don't say or do. Don't, for example, allow yourself to be photographed with a pint of beer in your hand – it will be just your luck that this is the very story and the very picture which are relayed round the country or the world.

Harvey, an American academic, researching issues of embodiment, had been doing body building for many years – in fact this leisure activity was what got him into his research in the first place. He won a major body building competition and he took the opportunity to place a story in the local media about his research. The local newspaper persuaded him to have a photograph taken in his office. He posed for them, wearing only his posing pouch and a mortar board, and the photograph was duly published in the local paper accompanied by a story that was less to do with his research than with his corporeality – as he would have put it. As if this wasn't embarrassing enough, the story was picked up by the national gutter press and the article and photograph were syndicated across the nation. Next, it was placed on a website and some of his colleagues overseas found it when they were looking for his email address using a search engine. Matters reached their apotheosis (or perhaps nadir) when it turned out that someone had pinned up a copy of the article and photo on the wall in the women's toilets next door to the (female) vice-chancellor's office. Dr Wallbanger was then summoned to the vice-chancellor's office to be disciplined.

Notwithstanding our cautionary tale, you shouldn't be deterred from trying to get your work known in and through the media. The idea is to practise and make perfect.

Now dive in the deep end

You are now well equipped to take the calls and the initiative and to do what is required with and for your media dissemination networks. Here are four possible scenarios and some handy hints.

Writing a column or story for the print media

This is the media form that comes closest to academic writing. Unlike other forms of media communication, writing your own article allows you to retain a significant level of control. Such writing may consist of opinion pieces, human interest stories or an account of your research for the newspaper or magazine audience. You will probably start by writing occasional columns but if you are good at it, you could become a regular contributor to a particular newspaper or magazine. Such pieces of writing vary in length, but are usually about 500–750 words. You should feel free to recycle your material. However, if you are in a country like the UK, which has a national press, you should not submit the same piece to, or publish it in, another newspaper. In contrast, in countries where newspapers are more locally or regionally based, like Australia and the USA, doing this is entirely acceptable. The key thing to think about is whether the two outlets are in competition with each other or not. Sometimes newspaper articles are syndicated nationally and even internationally, and it may a good idea to ask if this can happen with yours – always assuming that the subject matter would travel.

To maximise your chances of publication you should do the following things:

- Call the editor who oversees the particular area your work is about and discuss your ideas to find out whether they might be interested in you writing a piece. You could fax or email a background briefing about your work to the editor and ask if they are interested, but remember that they probably get even more emails each day than you do and are unlikely to take much notice of one from someone they have never worked with before, so this is a strategy better used when you have previously written for that editor or which your press officer could use in trying to place a piece by you.

- Once the editor has agreed to commission a piece, you need to negotiate how much you will be paid for it. They will usually offer you a standard amount.
- Remember you are engaged in a process of translating your ideas to new audiences, so write as simply as you can. Do not allow yourself to run away with your beautiful complex theories such that your lay readers can't understand what you are on about.
- Always begin with a bang and with your most important point. People generally read the first paragraph of a newspaper article with some attention, allow their concentration to slip with the second and skim the third. Also, if your piece is going to be cut by a sub-editor trying to get it into the space, they like to be able to just cut off the last couple of paragraphs and don't want to do the work of rewriting to tighten up your language.
- Be provocative, or, at least, be different or edgy in some way. You want people to find your piece interesting, but don't falsify or misrepresent your research in order to do so.
- Be relevant and timely. If you keep an eye on the news, or if you know about particular events likely to happen soon, such as the publication of a major government report relevant to your work, you will be able to time your writing for the press to fit in with what is topical.
- Overall, be newsworthy.

Katie was a well respected academic and an experienced editor of a major social science journal. The editorial team decided to create an offshoot from the journal in the form of a more popular magazine. This required Katie to develop new editorial skills and to commission and write articles for a more lay readership. She learnt these new skills rapidly and soon became adept at journalistic writing, without abandoning her high academic standards. She then thought she would turn her hand to generating some opinion pieces for newspapers. Although her message is not at all mainstream – indeed, it might be regarded as quite radical – she has become expert at ▶

▶ constructing her newspaper pieces in such a way that they are entertaining, persuasive and thought-provoking. Initially, she wrote occasional articles for the state press. Now, however, the press commissions her to write articles on all manner of topics.

Answering a request for information for a newspaper report

Sometimes a journalist will approach you in connection with an article they are writing. You need to be on your toes when you speak to them and not be seduced or flattered into saying things that you regret later. With this in mind, you should pay attention to the following things:

- When you get a phone call, on no account should you spend hours giving the journalist background information or agree to talk to her on the spot.
- Ask about her deadlines, when she expects her article to be published and what format it will take. Is it to be a news piece or an opinion piece? If she is a staffer there is stronger likelihood that it will be published but also that it will be a news item rather than a more extended discussion. If the journalist is freelance, then it is worth asking whether they have been commissioned to write the article already or whether they are planning to write it in the hope of selling it to someone. In the latter case the chances of not getting published are the highest. If the journalist's work has been commissioned, on the other hand, it will almost certainly be published – although the editor will still go through it with the metaphorical blue pencil. Make a judgement about whether the time you will spend talking to the journalist is worth your while.
- Ask the journalist what angle she takes on the issue, what story she is trying to tell and what questions she intends to ask you. This is another point at which you must make a judgement about whether it is worth your while. If the line she is taking is completely alien or offensive to you, then don't proceed any further. Don't get taken in. Remember that journalists are very good at making you feel you can trust them – it is one of their key professional skills.

- It's not a good idea to simply brush a journalist off, as that can form a negative part of her story. You should always appear to be helpful and if you feel you don't want to speak to her, for whatever reason, give her the names of some other people she could speak to instead and say politely that you haven't the time to talk at the moment – for example, you have a class waiting for you and are going abroad tomorrow. As soon as you put the phone down, however, you should contact the people whose names you've given out and warn them that they may be approached.

- If you do agree to talk to the journalist, arrange to have her call you back at a mutually convenient time and ask her to fax or email you with her questions in advance.

- In the meantime you may want to fax or email an abstract of your relevant papers or the executive summary of any pertinent reports you have written.

- Fax or email her your biographical statement and your media résumé. (It's good for journalists to have this on file.) Make sure she is clear that you want to be properly cited and to have your institution and your official title correctly attributed.

- Then do your nutshell exercise. You will thus have your central theme and key points ready when she calls. And, of course, you have a hook!

- When she calls back, keep focused on what you have prepared, the contact time short and your conversation to the point. Do not take the liberty of making any off-the-topic, off-the-cuff, off-the-record remarks unless and until you know the journalist well enough to feel confident that you can trust her implicitly.

- If the reporter is asking you to comment on work that you have done with colleagues, make sure that she mentions them in her report. If they are not mentioned there will be heaps of negative fall-out for you and your team.

- Ask to see a copy of the article before it is published or at least of what she plans to use of what you have said. However, whether they are prepared to do so or not will depend very much on local conventions. In the UK, for example, it would be very unusual for a journalist to agree, while in Australia she will probably be happy to do it, given sufficient time.

- Keep a file of your media clippings. Put the information in your CV next time you update it (which should be a regular event – *Building Your Academic Career*).

For the last two years Jeff has been involved with a major research project together with senior academics from another local university. The project has recently been completed and Jeff has contacted a journalist from the higher education press in order to try to get some coverage for the project's conclusions. In the course of the interview, Jeff talks about the project with pride and ownership and, unintentionally, completely forgets to mention his collaborators. When the story is published, it inevitably appears as if Jeff did the project on his own. His colleagues are incensed at being written out in this way. They know that it must be Jeff's fault because the journalist writing the article specialises in reporting research and knows very well the conventions of attribution.

Accepting an invitation to go on the radio

Radio interviews are a very different genre from those in the print press or on television. Academics often think that they will be easy, but in fact they are really difficult to do well. This is because listeners rarely give their full attention to the radio and nearly always listen with only half an ear while they do something else – washing up, driving, ironing and so on. This means that you have to be particularly crisp and clear, not only in what you say but also in how you say it. Don't mumble or speak in a monotone, for instance. It also means that you have to ensure that you draw vivid pictures with your words, sound lively and interesting so that you catch the audience's ear and make your points easy to follow. The only way to ensure that you are able to do this when a microphone is stuck in front of you is to practise, practise, practise.

When you are asked to do an interview on the radio (or television) the person who contacts you will be the programme's researcher, not the actual broadcaster. There are a number of things you need to do for a radio interview, in addition to the relevant points about press interviews.

- Ask about the radio format and audience. You can also ask about payment – they may pay if you ask but may not always offer. If there is no payment then you can make your own decision about whether you want to spare the time or not.

- Find out whether the interview is to go live to air or is to be pre-recorded. If the latter, you may be able hear the tape before it goes to air. If it goes out live, the advantage is that no-one can alter what you say or take it out of context. On the other hand, if you mess up, there's little you can do to fix it. Conversely, in recorded interviews you can ask to re-record your answer to a question – though perhaps not too frequently – if you feel you haven't responded clearly, but your words can be cut and slotted into a context in which they seem to say something you didn't mean.
- Find out when the interview is to be conducted, how long it will last, who is to conduct it and where it will take place. It may be in the studio or down the line (that is, on the phone or in a remote studio). It may be interesting for you to go to the studio to see how things are done and good to meet the interviewer as part of your networking – but it probably isn't worth spending a huge amount of time and effort getting there for an interview that lasts only a very few minutes. Agree to go to the station or studio only for an extended interview or if you want to do so for your own purposes. In some cases the broadcasting company will send a car for you, and this can considerably ease your travel problems – always ask about this.
- Find out whether you are the only guest. If not, ask who will accompany you. If it is someone whom you do not want to be interviewed alongside, refuse the invitation or ask for another time slot.
- Ask for the questions and particularly for the first question. It is always comforting to know how to start. Radio interviewers will generally be happy to give you the first question in advance, but may not be sure how they will follow up until they have heard your answer.
- Nutshell.
- Rehearse if this is one of your first few radio interviews.
- If you are going to a studio, then, when you arrive, the sound technicians will mike you up, check sound levels and so on. Whether the interview is down the line or at the studio, if you are to go live to air you will be put on hold for a while as the technical staff wait to cut to you and as the previous part of the programme winds up. This allows you to get a sense of the interviewer's style. You will also know more or less what to expect if you have previously listened to broadcasts by your interviewer.
- Attend the interview well prepared and with a little time to spare at the start.
- Keep to your agenda. Don't be tempted to go down all kinds of alleys proposed by the interviewer. If you are asked a question that

gets you away from the points you want to make, you can respond by saying something like 'Of course, the most important point to remember is ... ' and return to the point you want to make. Listen to how politicians do this when they are interviewed on news programmes – you may not want to emulate them, but they are usually adept at the craft.

- If a question does not make sense to you, then it's okay to ask for it to be rephrased. Or, perhaps even better, you could answer a question you want to have asked. For instance, you could introduce your answer by saying something like 'I think it is helpful to come to that issue from another angle.'

- If the interviewer is wrong, don't correct them automatically. If they have made a mistake that doesn't really matter – for instance, given you the wrong title – then correcting them not only makes you look pompous and petty but also gets in the way of what you actually want to say. Most news item interviews are for three minutes or less, and fifteen seconds taken up with an unimportant correction is simply a waste of time and a distraction from the real points that you want to make. On the other hand, if the interviewer's mistake is one of substance – for instance, they quote you as having said something diametrically opposed to what you believe – then it's appropriate to correct them politely, always taking care not to make them look foolish.

- Try for a killer ending. It is good to conclude the interview on your terms and in a memorable way.

Another radio genre you may be invited to participate in is the radio talk-back programme. This has some common features with the radio interview, but you will be responding to listeners' points, made in telephone calls, rather than to an interviewer. Such points may not necessarily be taken in any logical order and it may be hard to anticipate what kinds of question will be asked. Although calls are screened and callers may be interviewed briefly before being allowed on air, sometimes crazy and/or offensive people do get through the net, so you need to be prepared. Keep in mind what we have said about interviews, and also attend to the following matters:

- Be clear and firm about how you will be identified. The title Dr helps – though obviously you shouldn't claim it unless you genuinely have a doctorate.

- Do not accept the invitation unless you are quick on your feet and on top of your subject matter.
- Stay very focused. Do not allow yourself to be sidetracked from your main messages.
- Do not respond to attempts to bait or anger you.
- Be prepared to acknowledge that there are things you do not know but accompany the acknowledgement with an assertion of what you do know.
- Remain calm and courteous.

For our illustration, we return to the radio interview, since academics are more likely to be asked to do these than the talk-back programme.

Gisela, who studied the work of the German poet Goethe, was asked to participate in a serious arts programme. She prepared by going back to an academic paper she had written about one of his most complex poems and thought carefully about how she could capture her detailed, highly theorised argument for radio listeners. She summarised her argument in listener-friendly language, getting rid of as much technical jargon as she could. Then she chose some vivid illustrations from Goethe's writings and what was known of his life to inject into her argument. Finally, she made notes of the three most important points she wanted to get across and thought carefully about which of her illustrations would best support the points. After that she got her partner to interview her as a practice, using the questions that the radio researcher had primed her with. The actual interview was a wow – Gisela gained plaudits from people who had heard it, and it featured positively in the radio review columns of several serious newspapers. Subsequently Gisela has been invited to take part in many arts programmes on radio and, latterly, on television – indeed, it has become quite a nice little earner for her.

Tangling with television

A researcher may approach you from a television company asking for your help in a number of ways. They may want you to help them with background for a programme they are hoping or have been commissioned to make. They may be looking for people they can interview on screen in some kind of documentary programme. Or they may be from a news programme and looking for good people to interview as part of an item of the day's news. In a few cases you may be asked if you will write and front a whole series – and some academics have done very well out of this – but we are not going to talk about that here, as it will apply to such a small minority of people. Television is different from the radio: in some ways it is easier but it is also often more daunting. There are a number of things you have to bear in mind when tangling with television.

- In interviews you should follow the same general principles as those outlined for radio and newspaper interviews – be crisp and precise, avoid patronising language and jargon, use vivid examples, and so on. Preparation is all-important here too.
- Ask where they will be filming. If it is to be in your own space – say your office – then check that it is tidy and have them film with an uncluttered background behind you. Clutter is really distracting on screen – and it's particularly important to avoid having your favourite Mickey Mouse poster or your Elvis clock behind you, which will both distract the viewer and trivialise you. The most difficult situation is a down-the-line television interview from a remote studio. In that case you will be in an empty room with a television screen and a cameraperson. Your instinct will be to look at the screen when your interviewer is speaking and then to turn and face the camera when you respond. Unfortunately, the television screen is invariably to the side of the camera and looking from screen to camera and back just makes you look shifty. The audience doesn't necessarily know that you're not in the studio with the interviewer, and this very natural movement of your eyes and head can make you look completely untrustworthy. So you must look at the camera – and do so as if you were engaging with the interviewer, not with a fixed stare. You really have to practise beforehand – though, even if you have, it is difficult.
- Think about what you are going to wear if you are being filmed. White shirts and blouses cause problems for the camera, as do checked and striped ones. If you notice a strobe effect on someone

when you are watching television it will probably be because they are wearing a striped shirt. By the same token, don't wear anything fussy. Simple, plain, quite dark and fairly formal is best. If you wear earrings, make sure you are wearing neat studs and nothing that dangles and swings. Next time you watch someone with dangly earrings on television, notice how distracting they are. Do wear make-up, as the lights make you look very washed out without it. The studio may offer to make you up, and you should accept the offer – although it looks hideously overdone to you, their make-up people generally know what they need to do to make you look reasonable on camera. If they don't offer you make-up, then it's worth doing your own and overdoing it – yes, even if you are a straight man. If you've never made yourself up before, practise or get someone who has to help you. If you're not sure whether you will be offered make-up or not, put it on anyway, as the make-up people can easily deal with it. Check with someone (make-up person, presenter or floor manager) that your clothes are tidy immediately before filming starts. If you are suddenly called by a television news researcher and asked to appear on their programme that night you may need to rush home to change or to the shops to buy something new – but it's worth it. If you are in a period when you know that you may be called on at any moment you should dress for television every day without fail.

- If you are asked by a researcher to provide background information about a programme they are in process of making, it's fine to talk to them for a limited period – you don't want to offend. However, such conversations can turn into very long and time-consuming affairs. Remember that television production companies have money to spend on consultants, so don't be shy to say up front that you can give them half an hour or so, but if it becomes more than that they will need to pay you (or your university) a suitable consultancy fee.

- If you are asked to take part in a documentary, then be very careful indeed. Often researchers will tell you that they are taking a responsible line and will be respectful of your work. You can easily end up spending hours being interviewed and have only a few seconds of your interview included, completely out of context. This can make you look and feel very stupid indeed.

Francis still cringes at the memory of his experience of being interviewed for television – and so do his colleagues and friends on his behalf. A television researcher persuaded him that they were making a responsible documentary series in his specialist area. Francis was quite experienced in dealing with the media and confident that he would be able to handle the situation. He spent a long time speaking to the television researcher and the producer in advance and then travelled a hundred miles to be filmed in their studio, spending nearly three hours there. When the programme was aired, he was devastated to find that the tone was trivial, vulgar and sensationalist and that his painstaking and lengthy interview had been cannibalised in ways that completely distorted his message. He appeared for a total of approximately one minute, split between several snippets showing his talking head, in a programme that lasted about fifty minutes.

Felicity was an experienced academic working in controversial areas of social science. She had established a good relationship with people in one of the big television stations. She wanted to do some research that she thought could form the substance of an interesting and important television documentary and pitched the idea to the TV company. It agreed to fund her to research and participate in the making of her proposed programme, and assigned a producer to work with her. This meant that she had a significant degree of control over the direction of the programme, and the producer took responsibility for aesthetic and technical questions. The documentary was not only successful as a television programme but played a significant part in changing the points of view of policy makers in her area. The academic book and articles that she wrote based on the research for her television programme were well received by her academic peers.

And finally ...

This book has emphasised the importance of networking for academics. We have taken you through academic, stakeholder and dissemination networks. In all cases we have pointed to the benefits and dangers involved. We have also offered some practical strategies to help you become a skilled networker. If you take only one thing out of this book, it should be that successful interaction with other academics, stakeholders of all kinds and the media will be more likely if you regard all these people as professional colleagues and your networking as the give-and-take of professional courtesies.

Further Reading

Bivins, T. (1995) *Handbook for Public Relations*, Lincolnwood IL: NTC Business Books. This book is a practical guide for public relations writing and is aimed at both the professional and beginner. It addresses the key ideas of target audiences and newsworthiness for both print and electronic media. It covers writing media releases, newsletters, magazines and professional publications, as well as advice on media interviews. PR is about establishing and maintaining good relations with key publics (p. 2); summary of key processes to achieve success (p. 5, expanded on pp. 5–27); definitions of newsworthiness (pp. 33–4); questions to consider when writing for television or radio (pp. 40–1).

Blaxter, L., Hughes, C. and Tight, M. (1998) *The Academic Career Handbook*, Buckingham. Open University Press. This book argues that networking is one of five key activities of the academic. (The others are teaching, researching, writing and managing.) The book bases its suggestions on the trend in academia towards highly competitive contract work. The chapter on networks is well researched and covers the different types of network relevant to academic careers, these being conferences, seminars and societies. Although the authors write primarily for a UK readership, the advice and research on networks are applicable across a range of contexts. This is a well researched book with extensive annotated bibliographies on academic careers and related areas.

Fox, J. and Levin, J. (1993) *How to Work with the Media*, Newbury Park CA: Sage. This book argues that academics can use the media to broaden the impact of their work, to bridge the gap between academic and non-academic cultures and to raise their professional status and profile. However, working with the media may also entail problems. Academics may find that it involves a disproportionate commitment of time and energy and may lead to a loss of credibility in the eyes of colleagues. This book contains practical advice on dealing with a variety of media contexts: interviews for the news; talk shows and feature programmes; print media and opinion columns. The authors stress the importance of image as well as content in visual media contexts. The book is complemented by interviews with producers from electronic and print media who give their advice on how academics can successfully use the media. It also supplies excellent examples of media releases and media biographies.

Sadler, D.R. (1999) *Managing your Academic Career: Strategies for Success*, St Leonards NSW: Allen & Unwin. This book aims to assist early-career academics to plan and manage the main tasks of academic life. The book is written in the form of letters to hypothetical early-career academics, and as such locates its advice in the personal experience of the author, rather than an assessment of scholarly work done in this area. The book covers a broad range of strategies for early career academics, including time management, confronting bias, choosing referees, teaching and publishing. In establishing a personal academic network, through, for example, conference attendance, academics are forced to articulate their work over a range of contexts, and this process can be highly valuable for the researcher. One of the ways that academics can maximise the potential networks within their faculty is by establishing a publishing syndicate of four or five members who meet regularly to assist and encourage the production of articles.

Schumacher, D. (1992) *Get Funded! A Practical Guide for Scholars seeking Research Support from Business*, Newbury Park CA: Sage. Although this book is primarily concerned with gaining research support from business it contains much that is useful in terms of networking with industry. The book argues that successful partnerships depend on understanding business culture and the ability to communicate effectively using the dominant codes of that culture. The corporate perspective about research is informed by interviews with industry, and the university perspective is informed by debates around the role of universities and the ethics of industry linkage.

Winter, C. (1994) *Planning a Successful Conference*, Thousand Oaks CA: Sage. This book argues that organising a conference can be an excellent way of networking. The book lays out the basics for a successful conference based on the author's experience in addition to supplying some tips on promoting yourself and networking at other conferences. The author argues that there are four basic rules on planning a successful conference: put everything in writing; be flexible; plan thoroughly; expect the unexpected. Of particular importance for the conference organiser is the need to be clear about the purpose of the conference and how it will meet the needs of those attending. Chapters cover areas such as conference budgets, preparing programme schedules, promotion and marketing, on-site logistics and post-conference activities.

Websites

About PR dot com, http://www.aboutpr.com/. Has enterprise-oriented yet useful information on dealing with the media, writing a press release and other public relations concerns. One of a myriad of sites dealing with PR that can be found by searching 'public relations resources'.

Academy of Management, http://www.aomonline.org/. A leading professional association for management research and education in the US. Its on-line services include journal archives, conference calls and events and job placements.

American Association for Higher Education (AAHE), http://www.aahe.org/. A cross-disciplinary forum for academics interested in higher education issues. Contains information on conferences and related events.

American Council of Learned Societies, http://www.acls.org/. A private non-profit federation of sixty-six national scholarly organisations. Its mission is 'the advancement of humanistic studies in all fields of learning in the humanities and the social sciences and the maintenance and strengthening of relations among the national societies devoted to such studies'. Contains links to all affiliated societies.

Associations and Societies, http://www.health.library.mcgill.ca/resource/associat.htm#American. Maintained by McGill University, Canada, it lists associations relevant to the health sciences in the US and Canada.

Conference Alerts: Academic conferences world wide, http://www.conferencealerts.com/index.htm. Lists conferences by discipline or country. Includes conference information form Australasia, the US and Canada, Europe and the UK and South Africa. Also offers free e-mailed updates of conferences matching given interests.

Directory of UK Associations and Learned Societies in the Humanities and Social Sciences, http://www.britac.ac.uk/links/uksahss.html. A database managed by the British Academy with extensive list of UK associations in, for example, classical antiquity, modern languages, history of art and music, economics and economic history, psychology.

European Academy of Management, http://www.euram-online.org/aims.htm. Aims to be an open, international and multicultural European forum for networking and research in general management, strategy, corporate governance, organisational theory, organisational behaviour and decision making. Also contains information on conferences and job markets.

Grapevine, http://www.sosig.ac.uk/help/gv.html#1. A search engine and recourse site for social science researchers to publicise information about events, career development opportunities and professional colleagues. Use it to find conferences, events, organisations and societies relevant to social science research in the US, Europe, UK, and Australia.

Intellectual Property Law Resources, http://www.magna.com.au/~prfbrown/ip_links.html. A comprehensive resource site for IPR-related information. Includes searches relevant to Australia, New Zealand, the US, Canada, Europe, Japan, Spain and the Philippines. Includes links to the Moscow Patent Bureau. and other IP information and news groups.

JISCmail, http://www.jiscmail.ac.uk/. A mailing list service sponsored by the UK higher and further education communities, enabling members of any discipline to stay in touch and share information by e-mail or via the Web. The aim is to support topical discussion, wide collaboration and rapid communications.

Research Finder, http://rf.panopticsearch.com/search/search.cgi?collection-research. Provides an on-line gateway to find researchers and research capabilities in Australia's research organisations. Primarily targeted at researchers, investors and industry, both in Australia and overseas.

Scholarly Societies project, http://www.scholarly-societies.org/. Lists academic and professional societies throughout the world in the areas of arts and humanities, health sciences, business and economics and social sciences. Maintained by the University of Waterloo, Ontario.

Social Science Research Council, http://www.ssrc.org/. An independent, non-governmental, not-for-profit international organisation that seeks to advance social science throughout the world and supports research, education and scholarly exchange on every continent.

World Federation of Public Health Associations, http://www.apha.org/wfpha/about_wfpha.htm. An international non-governmental organisation bringing health workers throughout the world together for professional exchange, collaboration and action. The only worldwide professional society representing and serving the broad field of public health, as distinct from single disciplines or occupations. It enjoys official relations status with the World Health Organisation and maintains close ties with UNICEF and other international organisations.

Index

information *cont.*
  see also dissemination networks; knowledge
initiative (networker activity), 19, 40–41
insider knowledge, 38, 81–2
institutions (internal networks), 13, 38–40
intellectual capital, 17
intellectual property rights, 28–33, 68, 69
intellectual space, 9
internal networks, 13, 38–40
International Monetary Fund, 67
international networks, 9, 14–15
international travel, 58–9
interpersonal skills, 18
interviews
  for newspapers, 112–14
  for radio, 114–17
  for television, 117–20

journal editors, 49
journalists, 112–13

knowledge
  commercialisation, 12–13, 33, 37, 60–61, 62
  economies, 12, 28–9, 36
  insider, 38, 81–2
  managers, 95
  outsider, 81–2
  ownership, 28–33, 68, 69
  production, 12–13, 16, 17, 36, 62
  services, 63–4
  see also information

language
  of media, 107–8, 109, 111
  of presentations, 45
  professional development activities, 86
learn to nutshell, 108, 113, 115
lectures (by visiting scholars), 52–5
letters of support, 15
listening skills, 18
lobby groups, 16, 65, 66
local media, 109, 110
local networks, 9
low-profile media, 109

make-up (on television), 119
managerialism, 14
materials (intellectual property rights), 29–30, 33
media, 10, 96
  academics chosen by, 105–6
  clippings, 113
  ethical dimension, 25, 27, 28
  mediating, 106–20
  profile, 98–9, 100–101, 103–4
  releases, 109
  résumé, 107
  they contact you, 101–3
  you contact them, 103–4
media dissemination networks, 98, 110
  benefits of, 99–100
  disadvantages, 100–101
mediating the media, 106–20
mega-conference, 46, 47
mentoring, 9, 21, 41
meta-conference, 47
mini-conference, 54
money, *see* funding
multiple stakeholders, 62–3

name badges, 48
National Council of Voluntary Organisations, 64
national networks, 9
national press, 110
negotiation (education/training), 90–91
networkers (skills/abilities), 18–23
networking
  with academics, *see* academic networks
  basics, 12–23
  benefits, 13–17
  characteristics (poor networkers), 20–21
  in context, 12–13
  for dissemination, *see* dissemination networks
  ethics, 7–8, 24–8
  golden rules, 23
  intellectual property rights, 28–33, 68, 69
  perks and quirks, 17–18
  planning, 33–5
  skills/abilities, 18–23
  with stakeholders, *see* stakeholder networks